"A vivid day-by-day account of a trek in the Everest region of Nepal.. brutally honest.. makes you realize what is truly important in life. An all-out emotional tribute to the son I lost.. and a father's love song to his own son. I was one hundred percent confident the Livestrong wristband I gave to Gary would be left on the summit of Kala Patar. *We made it, Jon.*"

> — Tim Loden, long-time friend and business partner

"Profound, amazing. I was so moved by this journal. Sitting here drinking my morning coffee, thinking what a miniscule part of the world I am, that I have not experienced even a molecule of what life offers us. At the end, I sat there just crying. I could not stop."

> — Kathy Lebous, cancer survivor

"Great adventures are inner journeys—this one is dazzlingly so... an inspirational affirmation of the art of living, a beautiful ode to friendship and fatherhood. Tenderness, vulnerability, strength, and resilience—it's all here. Please commit more philosophy, Gary."

> — Dr. Leisha Emens, Assistant Professor of Oncology at Johns Hopkins University and climbing partner

"Having climbed two 19,400-foot mountains with Gary, I saw first-hand the pull the mountains had on him, and his desire to share them with his son, Michael. This beautifully written story is similar to what I witnessed on Kilimanjaro with them. It was there where Gary fulfilled his promise to make the Himalayas his last solo journey and helped get his son to that summit. What a storyteller and what a father! Can I come back as his son?"

— Andrew Buerger is the Founder of Jodi's Climb for Hope and the Director of Rare Earth Adventures. His book, *Carrying a Flag from Pain to Passion*, was the #1 new release on Amazon's Mountain Climbing books list

Chasing
Shangri-La

Chasing Shangri-La

*a soul-searching journey
to the Himalayas*

Gary Ingber

Apprentice
House Press
Loyola University Maryland

First Edition

Paperback ISBN: 978-1-62720-364-7
Ebook ISBN: 978-1-62720-365-4

Printed in the United States of America

Design by Sienna Whalen
Edited by Rosie DiTaranto
Promotion by Bri Rozzi
Map courtesy of Wilderness Travel

Published by Apprentice House Press

Apprentice
House Press
Loyola University Maryland

Loyola University Maryland
4501 N. Charles Street
Baltimore, MD 21210
410.617.5265
www.ApprenticeHouse.com
info@ApprenticeHouse.com

This journal is dedicated to two sons: to Jonathan Brett Loden, the son of my long-time friend, business partner, and blood brother, who fought with valor but died of head and neck cancer while I was in Nepal—and to my own son, Michael Benjamin Ingber, impossibly even more precious now, who will live to fight on and climb his own mountains.

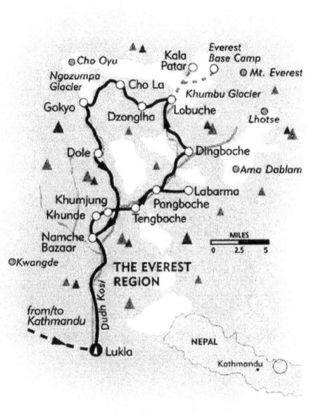

En route to Kathmandu

"K-k-k-k-Kathmandu
That's really, really where I'm going to
Oh, if I ever get out of here
I'm going to Kathmandu."
—*Bob Seger, lyrics to Kathmandu*

"There's still time, but there ain't forever."
— *Rick Sylvester, climber*

I owe you this one, Michael. I had promised you a Kilimanjaro journal when I climbed it in September 1998. But when I got back, the demands of everyday life took over and I never got it done. I'll make Kili up to you by taking you there next summer, but you're on your own for Nepal. I won't be taking you there. If you choose to follow in my footsteps one day, then let this journal be your guide.

..

Nobody ever said it was easy getting to Shangri-La. Five and a half hours Baltimore to Los Angeles, a two-hour layover at LAX, 17 hours LA to Bangkok, a four-hour layover at Don Muang, three and a half hours to Kathmandu, Nepal. Thirty-two non-stop hours of traveling.

I cashed in some frequent flyer miles for a first-class upgrade on the first leg to LA. A double Glenlivet, a glass of Viognier, and a good branzino led to a lot of reflection. I'm at a crossroads in my life. Six weeks ago, I resigned from the software company I founded and built for the past 27 years. Four years ago, I sold the company, running it since then under a consulting arrangement with the company that bought it. In retrospect, it's a bleeping miracle I lasted the four years. Hands tied, going nowhere, the thrill was gone. The last year, especially, was brutal. Bored and unchallenged, I found myself sleepwalking through life. It's time for waking up.

So here I am, 57 years old, thinking about the undone things in my life and searching for a way forward. Nepal is not a celebration. Far from it. It's a deliberation on everything that matters: where I stand and where I go from here.

Do the mountains hold redemption, transformation, some answers? Even if they don't, Tim, my long-time friend, business partner, and blood brother, has given me a purpose I can't ignore. His son Jonathan is in the end game after a two-and-a-half-year battle with head and neck cancer. Tim and I have stood by each other through some blinding shitstorms, but this time I've stood by helplessly watching the battle shatter Tim and Lollie's lives. Yesterday Tim met me for lunch and gave me a Lance Armstrong wristband. All choked up, he asked me to leave it on a summit for Jon. That looms large.

I jolt awake some mornings and think, "Oh my God, I'm 57." All right, so it's not as easy as it used to be. But I refuse to accept that I'm past it. They say it takes six months to get ready for this. I gave it six weeks. There wasn't much time left to catch the spring climbing season, and windows of opportunity have a way of slamming shut.

After two-a-day Krav Maga workouts, some dawn patrol trail running, some yoga, and with several long hikes thrown in, I feel physically and mentally tough enough to handle it. Emma overheard me kidding with Abby that I was "a lean, mean, fighting machine," and she said, "Zadie, you're not mean." Mean or not, ready or not, here I come.

The Himalayas are one of those undone things in my life. As a kid I must have seen the movie *Lost Horizon* ten times, and the Himalayas and the search for Shangri-La left me totally in awe. It was a dream I had given up, but my newfound freedom resurrected it. Me being me, I have to go for it.

Mom and your grandmothers are all aghast. They don't get it, and I can't explain it to them. How do you explain that mountain wanderlust is incurable? Or that yearning voice, deep down in all of us, that says, "Fuck it, I'm following my heart. I'm gone."

I got a wake-up call from your grandmother this morning. "You're crazy to do this and you're going to die," she said. "I know you are. How can you do this to me?"

"All right," I said. "If I'm going to die, then why don't you meet Iris, me, and the kids for lunch to say your last goodbyes."

"Oh no, I can't," Grandma replied. "I've got to get my hair done."

There's no explaining the deep pull of the mountains. You either feel it or you don't, and I feel sorry for those who don't.

At least I know you're proud of me for going. When you told me that, it meant more to me than I let you know. I hope you know how proud I am of you. You proved yourself to me last summer on Mt. Shasta. You even proved yourself to me as a little boy that Skyline Drive weekend when you fell off the horse, breaking your collarbone, when you had the courage to saddle yourself back up and ride all the way back in pain. I wish I could take you with me on this one, but pulling you out of school for a month just doesn't make sense. This will be my last solo adventure trip. From now on, you'll be with me. Maybe your sisters and brothers-in-law and maybe even your mother, too. But this is one I've got to do without you.

The Thai have *shibumi*. The 17-hour Thai Airways LA to Bangkok leg is full of that Thai effortless perfection. No domestic airline even comes close. Excellent service, three outstanding meals, three videos, and a couple of hours of light sleep. By the way, Thai women are exquisite. Your mother's got my body, heart, and soul in this life, but if the Buddhists are right about a next life, Thai women will be high on my list.

Mid-morning in the Bangkok airport, and I'm sitting at the gate writing this and waiting to catch that last leg to Kathmandu. I'm flying into a freaking mess. Nepal is convulsing with civil war. Maoist rebels are shaking down trekkers in the Annapurna region and blowing up buildings in the cities and towns when they're flush with explosives. In Kathmandu, a bunch of gonzo political parties are rivaling each other and protesting for democracy against a 240-year-old constitutional monarchy that's no longer constitutional since the king has disbanded the Parliament. At the moment, a planned peaceful four-day strike and protest has mushroomed into a belligerent 12 days of rioting, the violence countered with curfews, tear gas, rubber bullets, and at least four killed. The US State Department has issued a travel warning against going to Nepal and has given leave to the embassy personnel. But hey, look at the bright side—I could just be headed to work for another soulless day at the office.

Andrew Peacock, our trek leader, just walked up to me to introduce himself. A 6'2", 39-year-old Australian doctor still trying to figure it all out, his enthusiasm for the mountains is contagious and makes me wistful for lost youth and lost opportunities. He flew in from Brisbane, Australia last night, and we're on the same flight to Kathmandu. He's a great guy, and we like each other immediately.

We ask for window seats on the right-hand side of the plane for the best shot at the mountains, and we board the flight. They say your first views of the Himalayas will give you goosebumps, but it's cloudy and raining all the way into Kathmandu. The mountains remain shrouded in mystery.

It's mid-afternoon Tuesday when Andrew and I finally touch down in Kathmandu, two days ahead of the rest of our team. For me, 32 hours of traveling and a day lost crossing the international date line. Our passports tattooed, we grab our bags and catch a shuttle to the Shangri-La Hotel. Nice name and a pretty swanky hotel for Kathmandu. Driving is on the left, but it's chaos and any lane goes. I unpack, wander the lobby and grounds, meet Andrew for dinner in the hotel, get back to the room, and crash.

Kathmandu

*"Deep within us I think we know that we need
challenge and danger, and the risk and hurt that
will sometimes follow…Mountain climbing is not
the only way of dealing with an over-organized,
over-protected society. But it's one good way."*
—*Woodrow Wilson Sayre*

Catch-up eight-hour sleep, I wake up to a
5:30AM sunrise, the morning light streaming
into the room through the open curtains. I
drift awhile in the currents of sleep before
jumping in the shower at seven. When I
emerge, still toweling off, I'm startled to see a
black-faced monkey sitting on my fourth-floor
window ledge. He's probably after the fruit
bowl sitting on a table by the closed window.
The monkey and I see each other at the same
moment and both jump, but we stare each

other down for ten seconds before he runs away. Good morning, Kathmandu.

Great breakfast buffet on the patio of the hotel's Shambhala Garden café—granola with yogurt and fruit, scrambled eggs, grilled tomatoes, pancakes, excellent coffee. I had a light dinner last night, so I'm famished and eat well. Andrew joins me shortly after I start. We both read our copies of the local paper, *The Himalayan*, over breakfast.

"Day 13 of the strike," Andrew comments.

"Death toll now 18, no end in sight," I reply.

In another article, Palestinian jihadis are recruiting a new army of 70 suicide bombers ready to blow themselves up for Allah.

"Blimey religious fanatics," Andrew mutters.

"Blimey, psycho-killer religious fanatics," I add, smiling at the Aussie pejorative. But I get a sinking feeling, worrying about your trip to Israel this summer. It's a father's job to worry about 70 blimey, psycho-killer religious fanatics and the welfare of his son.

I head out alone for Thamel (pronounced TA-mel), the funky, frenetic tourist center of Kathmandu. It's about a 20 minute walk from the hotel in a light rain, but the rain has lifted the usual smog that envelopes the city. I pass stately embassies, closed with the protests, and the huge walled Royal Palace grounds of King Gyanendra. The king's not there—he's gotten out of Dodge—but there are young RNA (Royal Nepalese Army) soldiers everywhere in blue camo with ancient assault rifles slung over their shoulders

On March 29th, a few weeks before my arrival, there had been a solar eclipse over Kathmandu which, to the ancient astrologers, portended the overthrow of a ruler or king, but these soldiers don't look like they're buying into the loopy prognostications of whack jobs who fated everything on the alignment of the stars.

The rain lets up as I enter Thamel. It's quiet from the mayhem of the riots, a few Israeli kids decompressing from their IDF service, but no American kids thinking they're the next Jack Kerouac. Thamel is another world: narrow, shop-lined alley streets, cycle rickshaws and every kind of one, two, three, and four-wheeled vehicle imaginable, the occasional smell of incense in the air, and abject poverty everywhere. The sights and sounds and smells are welcome sensory overload. It's a kick. I wander the ancient streets, buying a flute for you from a street hustler and spending a lot of time buying a silk rug for Mom from a merchant who offers me tea and moans about how poor business is because of the strikes and curfews. You offer half of their asking price and start negotiating from there.

Back on the streets, I get hit on by a rail-thin Hindu mother with a baby in her arms who approaches me saying, "Baby is hungry." As I reach for my pocket, she says: "No money. Buy milk for me in market." That's pretty creative, I think, and follow her into the market. She quickly loads up, buying not just milk but packages of rice and cooking oil. The baby in her arms even points to a chocolate bar at the register. I smile at the con, nod my consent, and decline her dinner invitation. I've blown ten dollars in worse ways.

On the way back to the hotel, I'm hit on again by a boy of about eight or nine. He asks me where I'm from, then tells me everything he knows about the US. He knows a lot. We walk together for blocks. He asks me to name countries in Europe and fires back immediately with their capitals. How many American nine-year-olds could do that? Finally, when we walk by a market, he asks if I'll buy milk for his little sister. All right, so I'm a walking ATM here, but there's no other way to get rid of this kid. I buy the kid the milk and laugh at the huge smile on his face as he walks away.

Back at the hotel, I do a light workout in the little fitness center, catch some sun and read by the pool, then jump in the sauna for 15 minutes. After a quick shower, I catch a cab to Swayambhunath, the Monkey Temple, an ancient Buddhist *stupa* (temple) whose eyes, painted on the four cardinal points, keep watch over commanding views of the Kathmandu Valley. I climb 365 steep, monkey-lined steps (a tribe of rhebus monkeys, like the one in my window this morning, is permanently encamped here) and get to the top of a forested hilltop shrine where a pagoda atop an enormous white dome glows golden as I watch Buddhist monks perform a sunset ceremony. Chanting "*Om mani padme hum*" in deep, resonant voices, the "m" sounds vibrating, it's hypnotic and pretty cool.

I'm on full alert, but badasses are nowhere to be found on the long walk back to the Shangri-La. I stop at a little Japanese restaurant, order vegetable fried rice and a fruit juice, and eat well for about $1.50.

The night is cool, the moon hidden, as I walk the gardens in the back of the Shangri-La. I'm feeling loose and confident, enjoying the freedom of being alone in an exotic third world city and looking forward to what lies ahead. I call home at 9:30PM when I get back to the room—it's 11:30 in the morning your time. Good to hear Mom's voice—just want her to know I made it here alive and well. All in all, it's a good first day in Kathmandu. I'm tired when I hit the bed at ten.

Thursday, April 20, 2006

Kathmandu

"I always go with people who can catch me."
—*Tom Brokaw, TV journalist and climber*

There's a shoot-on-sight, all day curfew today
and I'm under orders to stay on the hotel
grounds. Not much choice anyway, the hotel
has its security gate up, locked, and manned
with an armed guard. So it's a day of winging
it in the Shangri-La. I linger at breakfast, read
The Himalayan from cover to cover, lounge at
the pool, read my weird Keith Cymry under-
ground novel, *Hope In A Nutshell*, workout at
the fitness center, and wait for the rest of our
team to arrive. They do around 1:30PM.

With the curfew all roads are closed to
traffic except tourist buses to and from the airport, and there are not too many of them. I'm

out-front wandering in and out of the shops on the hotel grounds when our group's shuttle pulls up with the big "TOURIST BUS" sign in its front window.

We introduce ourselves over complimentary rum and orange juice drinks from the hotel. I get a pretty good feeling about the team. They say that mountaineers are bands of brothers, all one party on one rope. Not sure I'd go to war with any of them, but I get the sense we'll be all right.

Jeff and Steve are a father/son team from California. Jeff is a 6'8", 48-year-old financial guy who does triathlons. Steve, 23, his speech laced with West Coast dude-isms, is just out of college, running a Peets coffee shop. My tent-mate Mark is a 53-year-old cerebral, somewhat wonkish research scientist from Washington State. Brent is a 39-year-old, super-talkative, super-friendly guy from east Tennessee who does public relations work and a lot of hiking in the Great Smoky Mountains. Carolyn and Billie Jean are 58 and 59, from Boca Raton, Florida and have done a lot of this stuff together. The team is experienced: six out of seven of us have climbed Kilimanjaro, several have done the Inca Trail, Jeff and Steve have climbed Shasta and done the John Muir Trail, the women have done a lot of 14ers in Colorado. Everyone is in good shape and knows what they're getting into.

I show Mark up to our room and leave him alone to unpack and rest up. We're meeting together later as a group for dinner.

I go to the business center to check emails and then to the garden cafe and order a chocolate shake. Back to the pool, another light workout, shower and change, and I meet the team in the garden for a 6:00 PM orientation dinner meeting. We go around the table and give our reasons for doing the trek.

"When it feels like you no longer have a pair," I begin, "it's time to shake it up."

I tick off my soul-crushing work situation, my sudden walk away, and the *Lost Horizon* childhood dream that had come surging back.

"I've come to reset, to get clean, to find the light again," I end.

Brent notices the yellow Livestrong wristband I'm wearing and asks, "Why the Lance Armstrong band?"

I nod and tell the team about Jonathan and Tim. "Somewhere on the trek, we'll be leaving the wristband together on a summit for Jon," I finish.

I can see the impact of the moment on the faces of my teammates. Dinner is an Indian buffet on the garden grounds under a harboring night sky. Everyone is pretty fried from traveling. We have an early morning city tour scheduled, and I think we're all crashed by nine.

Friday, April 21, 2006

Kathmandu

*"Do what thy manhood bids thee do. He noblest
lives and noblest dies who makes and keeps his self-
made laws."*
*—Sir Richard Francis Burton, British explorer,
1821-1890*

The curfew is lifted in time for us to do
a 6:30AM trip to the Buddhist Stupa at
Boudhanath, a massive, towering temple. On
the road there, Andrew, Jeff, and I have to get
out of the shuttle bus several times to move
concrete blocks that were lane dividers but
have been knocked down by the protesters to
block off the street.

Early morning is the perfect time of day
to be at the temple to see the monks and the
local Nepalis begin their early *kora*, their ritual

clockwise circumambulations around the temple. Jeff, Steve, and I climb to the top of the temple where the Buddha's eyes, known as "Judgment Eyes," ominously gaze out from a square base of spire where thousands of pigeons gather. I spin the prayer wheels at the top, figuring we'll need all the help we can get.

Back on the street, I buy a postcard of the Judgment Eyes to send to you and Mom. I also buy some Tibetan bread from a street vendor and am immediately surrounded by three kids. I break off hunks of bread for the kids and get back thousand-watt smiles in return.

We're back at the hotel by 9:00 AM in time for breakfast and the next curfew-bound day. I take my time over an omelet and fruit breakfast, lounging around and bonding with everyone. Andrew arranges for us to watch two videos after breakfast.

The first video is all about the symptoms and dangers of AMS (Acute Mountain Sickness) and what happens if you go too high, too soon—HACE (High Altitude Cerebral Edema) and HAPE (High Altitude

Pulmonary Edema) which can both kill you if you don't go down. Andrew jokes that there's a third phenomenon to watch out for at altitude—HAFE, High Altitude Flatulence Experience, and he's on target with that as several of our team later experience first-hand on the trek.

The AMS video leads to a discussion on Diamox. Andrew is pretty convincing that with our itinerary geared to acclimatization, we won't need it. I've already had this discussion with him one-on-one, and he knows I'll be taking it. After witnessing the effects of mild and severe AMS on my climbing partners on Kilimanjaro, the Grand Teton, and Shasta, I know I don't want to go there. I've come to believe in "better climbing through chemistry." Andrew has asked me to keep it to myself, and I respect his wishes.

The second video, *Himalaya*, is a beautiful film about a remote village of yak herders crossing a mountain pass to get their salt to market. The Dolpo people do phenomenal acting jobs, the soundtrack is mesmerizing, and the Himalayan mountainscapes are staggering. I feel mountain fever coming on. One of the lines from the movie sticks with me for the rest of the trek: "Whenever life presents you with two paths, choose the harder one."

Lunch, more pool time, another workout. Writing this, I'm drinking a chocolate shake in the garden (they're addictive) and worrying that we'll be shut out of our flight to Lukla tomorrow morning to start the trek. We're up against two problems. Domestic flights have been cancelled with the curfews, and since the airstrip in Lukla is a nosedive sight landing, we'll also need clear weather for take-off. Boredom is setting in, and I'm more than ready to get to the mountains. When we get out of Kathmandu and into the Solo Khumbu (the Everest trekking region), we'll be immune from the political situation. Getting there is the trick.

The sun sinks through a reef of clouds as Andrew and I catch a dinner of *momos* (dumplings stuffed with vegetables and chicken) on the patio of the garden café. I head up to the room to pack my expedition bag and back-pack, settle my bill at the front desk, and leave a duffel at the bell desk with the gifts I bought and some clean clothes for our return after the trek. Nothing left to do but call Mom to say I love her and good-bye for the next 20 days. If we catch the Lukla flight tomorrow, I'll be off the grid and incommunicado until we get back to Kathmandu.

Lukla (9,350') to Tok Tok (8,660')

"It is wonderful to be back. Back among mountains that remind us of our vulnerability, our ultimate lack of control over the world we live in. Mountains that demand humility and yield so much power in return."
—*Alex Lowe*

Our luck is changing. Up at 4:00AM, a quick breakfast, and we're off to Tribhuvan airport to catch the first flight to Lukla. "The mountains are calling," Andrew says, "and we must go."

The Lukla flights are notoriously delayed because weather conditions need to be right for the nosedive sight landing on the little mountain airstrip. But the weather this morning is perfect. We're on a 12-seater Yeti

Airlines prop plane, the front seats of the plane piled high with our duffels and backpacks. The 40-minute flight northeast to the beginning of the Everest trekking region is jaw-dropping. We catch our first views of the Himalayas, I get goosebumps, and I'm starting to feel like this is the real deal.

I shoulder my pack as we climb above the airstrip to meet our Sherpa crew, porters, and yaks. Our *sirdar*, head Sherpa and co-leader, is named Pemba, who proves to be rock-solid and reliable. He's flanked by the inscrutable Zomba, the always helpful Lakpah, the ever-smiling Sonchai, our very capable cook, Pemba Tzering, two beautiful Sherpani yak herders, and a host of porters and cook boys—17 in all to support our team of eight. Kind of embarrassing but there's no way we're making this without Sherpa support. Besides, it feels good to do our part in supporting the Sherpa economy.

The Sherpas are a mountain people, physiologically adapted to high altitude, hardworking, affable, and intelligent—the kind of guys

I would go to war with. Devoutly Buddhist, often chanting and rolling their prayer beads, they migrated south from Tibet to the Everest region four or five centuries ago. Climbing and trekking Sherpas enjoy great esteem in their communities—they can earn $2,000-$2,500 for two months in each of the two trekking seasons, attractive pay in a country mired in grinding poverty with an annual per capita income of around $200. They serve us "hot lemon" (hot lemonade) while our gear is loaded onto yaks, big shaggy beasts with mournful faces. The yaks are technically *dzopkyos*, male crossbreeds of yak and cattle, and *dzom*, female crossbreeds, but Westerners have a hard time discriminating and just call them all yaks. Yak bells on the trail strike a soothing chord that lingers in the air like distant wind chimes, but yak horns can be a little disconcerting. Just remember to always stay on the uphill side of the horns as you pass on the trail. Porters also carry a lot of our gear in straw baskets, enormous loads on their backs supported by straps around their foreheads, their neck muscles bearing the brunt of the weight—all for $3 a day. You've got to have a Buddhist outlook on life to be a porter.

It's mid-morning before we're all packed up, Andrew gives out a "*Johnny-Ho*" (Nepali for "Let's go"), and we're off.

From Lukla, the trail heads north through the deep gorge of the Dudh Kosi, the "Milk River," a boulder-strewn river which runs almost white with glacial runoff. We're in the Solo Khumbu now (just Khumbu for short), the Everest trekking region, which is a handful of valleys draining the southern slopes of Mount Everest, a small, starkly rugged region completely devoid of roads, cars, or wheeled vehicles of any kind. The trail is easy and mostly downhill at the start. I'm behind Sonchai, leading our group. With just a backpack holding little more than rain gear, a fleece jacket, some water, a few candy bars, and my camera, I'm feeling unburdened and unhurried, caught up in the simple joy of walking in exotic country.

The trail is relatively quiet—the political

unrest in Nepal has cut deeply into tourism and trekking the last several years—but there are occasional trekkers coming the other way, some looking a little hammered and dazed and confused after their long trek. There are also some yak trains, red-robed monks, and barefoot or sandal-clad porters straining beneath back-breaking loads. The trail greeting is "*Namaste*" (nam-as-STAY), Nepali for something like "I salute the God in you", and everyone on the trail is very cordial.

The spectacularly fluted ice pinnacles of Thamserku and Kusum Kangra pierce the sky more than two vertical miles above us as we make our way down the river valley, crossing the Dudh Kosi several times over suspension bridges, skipping along from one Sherpa village to the next—Chablung, Ghat, Phakding. Beyond the bridges, the dirt path abandons the banks of the Dudh Kosi and zigzags up steep canyon walls, cascading through aromatic strands of pine.

It's magnificent country, a geological crash site caused by India running into Asia, but it's not wilderness and hasn't been for centuries. Every scrap of arable land has been terraced and planted with barley, buckwheat, and potatoes. Rock-walled yak corrals line the landscape. Strings of prayer flags are strung across the hillsides. Ancient Buddhist *chortens* (religious monuments made of rock containing sacred relics, also called *stupas*) and walls of exquisitely carved *mani* stones greet you and stand sentinel as you crest the highest passes. *Mani* stones are small, flat rocks that have been meticulously carved with Sanskrit symbols denoting the Tibetan Buddhist mantra "*Om mani padme hum*" (literally "Behold the jewel in the lotus"). They are piled along the middle of the trail to form long, low *mani* walls. Tradition dictates that you pass *mani* walls on the left as you chant the mantra. Steve has gotten ahead of me and blows this several times, and I gently chide him. In one of the villages a little boy hands me a flower, then touches my pocket. I smile and give him 20 rupees.

It's an easy day, only about three and

a half hours of trekking with a long lunch break at a lodge at the top of a crest. It's about 3:30PM when we reach our campsite at Tok Tok, a peaceful spot with 360-degree views by a cascading waterfall.

Some of the Sherpas have gotten ahead of us, and our tents are already set up. We have popcorn and afternoon tea, I sort out my tent, then take a walk alone, first below our camp, back to the waterfall, and then above our camp to the crest of the next hill. The high Himalaya opens up before me, and I'm awestruck. It's so good to be back in the mountains. I gaze out and get choked up thinking of Jon. Here I am, running wild and free, dharma bumming in the middle of God's country, while Jon is facing the end and strug-gling for every breath. *We're in this together,* I tell Jon, *and we'll make it together.*

Dinner is *daal bhat,* the traditional Sherpa meal of rice with lentils on top, and Sherpa tea. We eat in a grim little stone building that is next to our campsite. Andrew gives us a briefing for tomorrow. It'll be a tougher day, our first real challenge as we take on the Namche Hill to get to Namche Bazaar, with an altitude gain of 2,640 feet. Andrew cautions us to take it easy. "If there's one day when you want to go slow and acclimatize, tomorrow is it." It's damp by the waterfall and the air takes on a wintry sting as night falls. Mark and I are in our two-man tent, bundled in our double sleeping bags by 8:30. I fade away to the rustle of wind over the short grass.

Namche Bazaar (11,300')

*"To venture causes anxiety, but not to venture is
to lose one's self... And to venture in the highest is
precisely to become conscious of one's self."*
—Soren Kierkegaard, Danish philosopher,
1813-1855

*"I've stumbled on the side of twelve misty
mountains."*
—Bob Dylan, A Hard Rain's a Gonna Fall

Shit happens. I had the runs last night. My
money's on the Sherpa tea, a half tea, half yak
milk combination. No pasteurization here,
and our Western bodies have no built-up
immunity. So, it was back and forth from
tent to toilet tent three times until there was

nothing left inside of me. The only consolation was a night sky electric with stars. By the end of the trek, six of the eight of us get hit with it. I'm just the first.

At 6:00 AM Pemba Tzering and his deep voice greet me with the first of many "Good mornings" and "bed teas" in our tent. I skip breakfast.

After tossing my packed duffel out of the tent, Brent and I start out ahead of the group, continuing up the Dudh Kosi gorge. It's a rolling trail, some ups and downs, on a clear, crisp morning with a glaze of frost sparkling on the rhododendron leaves, but when the sun rises above the canyon walls, the temperature soars. I layer down to a long sleeve T-shirt rolled up to my elbows after the first half hour. The mountains are spectacular as the sun lights them up, and around every bend a knockout view opens up. The peak of Thamerserku gleams in the morning sunlight. Brent aptly calls the trail a "stairway to heaven."

We're again skipping like a stone from one Sherpa village to the next—Benkar then

Chomoa—dodging yak dung all along the way. The Sherpas say it's good luck to step in it, better luck not to.

We watch the villagers open up their shops calling out "*Namaste, namaste*" to us. From Chomoa, the trail climbs to the Riverside Lodge, then descends steeply into a big valley below Thamserku. The trail crosses the Kyashar Khola across a long suspension bridge where we have to wait out a long yak train and then climbs out of the valley to Monjo.

Brent dodges off the trail for a pit stop, and after waiting out another long yak train at the top of some stone steps, I continue alone to Monjo, where we've agreed to meet up. I'm sitting on a low stone wall, the sun on my face, when Pemba pulls up, a warm smile on his face. The rest of the team is not far behind.

Together we climb to the hilltop school in Monjo and watch the Sherpa kids play in the dirt school yard before the bell rings at 10:00 AM. The kids are adorable.

Just beyond Monjo, the trail enters the

Sagarmatha (the Nepali word for Everest, "Goddess of the Sky") National Park. Pemba has collected our entrance permits. While we pose for the photo op under the entrance sign, Pemba hands our permits to the machine-gun-toting army rangers who man the park entrance station, record our arrival in a log-book, and then return the permits to us.

Beyond the park entrance, the trail makes a steep rocky descent to a large farm, then turns left at a cluster of buildings at the bottom of the hill, crosses the Dudh Kosi again on a high, long suspension bridge (I think there are 11 bridge crossings), and then follows the west bank of the river. A short dis-tance up the river is Jorsale. We detour around yaks and crowds of porters hanging around the village.

After following the river for a while, we stop for lunch high above the riverbank. I try eating some *chapati* bread with apricot jam, but I can't keep it in, and within five minutes I'm ducking behind some boulders.

We continue following the river on a

pretty trail and recross the Dudh Kosi. After a few ups and downs, we make a steep climb near the confluence of two rivers—the Bhote Kosi from the west and the Dudh Kosi from the east. A set of steep, crooked concrete steps, then the trail crosses the Dudh Kosi one more time on a suspension bridge that's a dizzying height above the raging river, the roar of the river billowing up in waves around us. Then begins a hard and steep three-hour ascent up Namche Hill which switchbacks up a dark, lush-forested hillside to Namche Bazaar.

Halfway up the ascent we catch our first glimpse of Everest through the clouds. Its unmistakable black wedge of summit pyramid stands out in stark relief, towering over the Lhotse-Nuptse wall, and sends out a plume of ice crystals that trails to the east like a long silk scarf.

I should be pumped, but with a sleepless night and no food, I'm running on empty and starting to fall behind the group. Legs heavy, head heavy, body older. The uphill is unrelenting, the switchbacks just keep coming. I can't find my uphill rhythm, and I'm hurting. *C'mon, I am not this old. No way it's caught up to me yet. I can do this.* I think I hear God snickering.

At a welcome rest stop at the crest of the switchbacks, I catch up with the team. There's a viewpoint of Everest, but the sky has clouded and there is no view. I talk to a Dutch couple, making their way downhill from Namche. They made it to Everest Base Camp but were unable to summit Kala Patar because of a deep snowfall. You never know when a fierce storm will slam into the mountains. You're in the hands of the mountain gods, and you summit at their mercy.

We continue on for the last push to Namche, and I continue to struggle. *One step at a time, pole, pole, bistaray, bistaray* (Swahili and Nepali for slowly, slowly). I'm going it on sheer determination now, lockstepping every step of the way to minimize fatigue in my leg muscles. Pemba and Sonchai are hanging back with me. We crest a broad ridge and are stopped at an RNA (Royal Nepalese

Army) checkpoint for several minutes while the guards grill Pemba and check his ID. He's talking Nepali but I make out the word "American".

Keep moving. I catch up with our group, sitting on a wall outside a tea house with rhododendrons in their hands. A little kid comes out to give me one, too. We're on the outskirts of Namche Bazaar, the social, administrative, and commercial center of the region.

We finally make it into Namche, and it's a pretty dramatic sight. Situated 11,300 feet above sea level, Namche sits in a huge, tilting bowl, like a tiered amphitheater, midway up a precipitous mountainside. More than 100 white-walled buildings with multi-colored roofs nestle dramatically on the rocky slope, linked by a maze of narrow paths and catwalks. It's an amazing place to be.

After winding our way up endless sets of stone steps, Sonchai and I finally arrive at the Panorama Lodge, a comfortable and welcoming Sherpa lodge, almost at the top of Namche. I'm wiped. I check into our room, wash up, and at 4:00 PM join the team in the glass-enclosed dining room for tea and French fries (Andrew calls them chips and so do I by the end of the trek). Loaded with salt and ketchup, the chips are irresistible. It's reckless, but my hunger wins out.

I catch up on my journal notes while I take in the friendly chatter of Swiss, Dutch, and Belgian trekkers all around me. The dreamlike maze of Namche fans out below until clouds roll in and whiteout our view.

Yak steak tonight for dinner above the clouds with a warm yak dung-fueled fire in the iron stove in the middle of the dining room. We refill our Nalgene bottles with water the Sherpas have boiled for us and make our way up to our rooms. I gutted out a tough day and am looking forward to sleeping hard tonight.

Monday, April 24, 2006

Exploration Day, Namche Bazaar (11,300')

"For a time, I rest in the grace of the world, and am free."
—Wendell Berry, "Peace of Wild Things"

Rough night. Woke up around 11PM with the runs again. Three trips later, I'm purged. Got to count those blessings—at least I'm in a comfortable lodge with a real bathroom and a Western toilet. My symptoms are not severe, and Andrew's medical opinion is just to let the gastro-intestinal bug run its course (weak pun, Doc). I'll fast today and give my body a chance to recover. If this is going to be a spiritual journey, I may as well go all in.

This is a needed rest, exploration, and acclimatization day in Namche. We meet in the dining room at 5:30AM to make a sunrise vista, but it's raining this morning, so we scrap the plans and go back to bed.

Breakfast at seven for everyone but me. It's cleared and we go off on a ridge hike high above Namche. The mountain scenery is spectacular as we conga-line along the ridge. At one point, we round a bend and I'm stopped cold. Two thousand feet below, the Dudh Kosi we crossed yesterday appears as a crooked strand of silver glinting in the shadows. Ten thousand feet above, the huge white fang of Ama Dablam hovers over the head of the valley like an apparition. It's a breathtaking mountain. And 7,000 feet higher still, dwarfing Ama Dablam, is the desolate, icy thrust of Everest, almost hidden behind Nuptse, with the usual horizontal plume of ice spewing from its summit. The summit looks so cold, so high, so impossibly far away.

My emotions swing from awe and wonder to a nervous anticipation of what lies ahead.

Andrew reminds us we'll be getting to Ama Dablam base camp in a couple of days for what he calls a "ripper" view (you've got to love the Aussie expressions).

We visit the Namche *gompa* (monastery) and continue on a fairly level hike heading west through glades of juniper, dwarf birch, and blue pine to the village of Thamo and back. There are carved *mani* stones all along the way. The Valkyrian skyline above bristles with the jagged snowcapped peaks I've been yearning for since I was a child.

A light rain begins to fall when we get to a ridgetop with a large *chorten* and prayer flags flying just outside of Thamo. We put on our rain gear and continue on to the village of Thamo, stopping at a lodge for a lunch I don't eat. The light rain continues to fall and it's a heads-down, just-go-for-it slog back to Namche.

The clouds clear. At the huge *mani* stone with elaborate white Sanskrit writings that hovers above the town, we hang a right and wind our way down to downtown Namche

Bazaar, a funky collection of several stone-covered streets lined with shops and restaurants. It's pretty cool to see yaks ambling down the shop-lined main street.

Worried about hitting snow later on, I buy a pair of $3 gaiters at one of the gear shops. Knock-off North Face and Mountain Hardwear gear is everywhere at prices too good to be true. We stop at the Hermann Helmer's bakery where Andrew, Steve, and Jeff load up on chocolate donuts. I buy a cinnamon roll which I wrap and stuff in my pack for a treat later on in the trek.

When you see Namche Bazaar, you can almost understand why a lot of visitors to the Khumbu are saddened by the boom in tourism and the change it has wrought in what early Western climbers regarded as an earthly paradise, a real-life Shangri-La. Entire valleys have been denuded of trees to meet the increased demands for construction and firewood. Teens hanging out in Namche carrom and pool parlors are wearing blue jeans and North Face and Mountain Hardwear jackets rather than quaint traditional robes, but the Sherpas don't bemoan the changes. They have no desire to be severed from the modern world or be preserved as specimens in an anthropological museum. Like our head Sherpa Pemba, they'd rather send their kids to expensive boarding schools in Kathmandu, and they've got no problem with the "*Video Night in Kathmandu*" phenomenon. We need to give up on our idyllic Shangri-La visions, and let the Sherpas get on with their lives.

It's a tiring climb up the endless steps of the mountainside amphitheater back to the Panorama Lodge where I catch a welcome outdoor shower for 200 rupees. After a 24 hour fast, I get a few bites of dinner down. Lakpah, the motherly Sherpani woman who owns the lodge with her husband, shows us *thanka* (pronounced TON-ka) paint-ings, hand-painted by her brother, who is a Buddhist monk. They're excellent work, and I buy one of the Tengboche Monastery, where we're headed in a couple of days.

I get into bed in the room in our lodge,

warm in my sleeping bag under a soft Sherpa fleece blanket, as Jon is waking to his 33rd birthday. I know inside it will be his last.

Khumjung (12,450')/ Khunde (12,600')

"The most beautiful and profound emotion we can experience is the sensation of the mystical. It is the source of all true science and art. He to whom this emotion is a stranger, who can no longer wonder and stand rapt in awe, is as good as dead."
—Albert Einstein

Scrambled egg breakfast which goes right through me (I should get this by now), then we climb to the top of Namche to the overlook we got rained out of yesterday morning. The 360-degree views are phenomenal, ridge after ridge of the great peaks of the Khumbu. Flanked by Nuptse and Lhotse, Everest shimmers far in the distance.

We sign in at a police checkpoint and visit

the Sagarmatha National Park Visitors Center and Museum. There are displays about the Sherpa people and their customs, the wildlife, mountaineering, and the impact of tourism. It's worth a visit.

The Sherpas believe the Khumbu region is a sacred place given to them by Guru Rinpoche, the founder of Buddhism, and is a place of refuge to go in times of trouble. I'm in complete agreement. The Sherpas also believe that you are reborn 42 days after you die. I smile at that. Forty-two days is six weeks, the exact amount of time between walking away from my business and coming to Nepal.

Leaving the visitors center, we start the trek northeast up to Khumjung, the Khumbu's largest village, about 1,500 feet above Namche. We hit some fierce uphills, I still can't find my uphill rhythm, and in my weakened condition, it's hard going.

We follow some kids on the way to the Hillary "School in the Clouds" and finally level off at the Shyangboche airstrip, built by the Japanese to service the nearby Hotel Everest View. The trail crosses the west end of the runway towards a telephone relay tower and the intersection of three trails. We follow the direct route to Khumjung, climbing past a *chorten* atop a ridge at 12,500 feet.

As we approach Khumjung, we reach a large side valley to the south. Beyond a *mani* wall and some picturesque *chortens* are the extensive grounds of the Khumjung school, the original Hillary school established in 1960. After summiting Everest in 1953, Sir Edmund Hillary felt greatly indebted to the Sherpa people. When he asked them what they wanted in return, they replied "schools and hospitals", and that's what he gave them.

About 15 kids of varying ages are playing cricket in the large dirt schoolyard. They're not doing well. Andrew and I make eye contact and go out on the field to show them how it's done. They're all laughter as Andrew takes the mound and I take the plate, holding the cricket bat, in bad form, like a baseball bat. When the first pitch comes in on a waist-high bounce, I step into it and crush a screamer about 300 feet to right field, or whatever it's called on a cricket field. Andrew calls out, "Well done, mate", and I jokingly reply: "And that's without steroids. The autograph line forms here." The kids probably don't understand a word I'm saying, but they're all laughing with me. I flip the bat to the closest kid, figuring I better get out while I'm ahead.

Alongside the trail, just beyond the school and besides a stream which runs right through the middle of the village, is the Ama Dablam Lodge where we set up camp for the night. The sacred peak of Khumbila rises above us. The Sherpas believe it is the home of the patron god of the Khumbu. The sky is threatening, and I feel my mood changing with the weather.

I can't keep lunch down, and when the rest of the team goes to visit the Hillary Hospital in nearby Khunde, I crash in the tent for a while. I rest but can't sleep.

I get out of the tent and follow a circuitous route up several terraces along the stone walls of the village, past a cedar grove, to the Khumjung *gompa* which I've read has an alleged yeti scalp on display. Hillary took this scalp to the United States for examination by scientists in 1960, and it was concluded that the scalp was made from the skin of a serow, a member of the antelope family.

But the yeti legend lives on. There is a haunting legend of a mystical Himalayan kingdom called Shambhala (In *Lost Horizon*, James Hilton transfixed the world and called it Shangri-La), a sacred kingdom where enlightenment and harmony reign and people enjoy extraordinary longevity. Surrounded by rings of mountains, the *beyul*, the fabled hidden land, can only be found by the worthy. Tibetan lamas believe it is guarded by giant snowmen who have acquired superhuman powers on the path to enlightenment. It is said they can bound at great speed and materialize and disappear at will. Many Sherpas claim to have seen yeti and many world-class climbers like Reinhold Messner confirm their sightings. Then again, Reinhold is a quasi-mystic who has spent a lot of time in the death zone, above 25,000 feet without oxygen, and has lost a lot of brain cells. The scalp in the Khumjung monastery looks like thin parchment with some hair growing out of it, and after leaving a donation, I conclude that it'll take a yeti sighting for me to become a believer.

I catch up with the group as I'm walking back to camp, and we all walk together to Pemba Tzering's (our cook's) house for 4:00 PM tea. It's cloudy and overcast and the house is gloomy in the late afternoon light. Pemba and his daughter Andiki's (one of our yak herders) hospitality is incredibly warm, but I'm feeling like shit. He serves Sherpa tea but when he sees that I'm not drinking it, he brings me black tea. He also serves little baked potatoes, and not wanting to insult him, I try one. Big mistake. When we get back to camp, I lose that, too, and collapse in my sleeping bag, all layered up, but shivering with chills. I stay in the bag through dinner. Andrew is concerned. He relents with the anti-medicine attitude and brings me an antibiotic called Microflux which he instructs me to take morning and night for three days. After suffering for almost four days, I'm in no position to argue. I pop one of the pills and try to sleep. But sleep is again elusive. I lie awake, listening to the night breathe.

Around 2:00 AM I'm still sleepless in Khumjung. Some nagging self-doubts are creeping in, and I'm starting to question whether I can make it all the way through this. I shake off the doubts, remember Jonathan, tell myself to cowboy the fuck up, and climb out of the tent.

Deep night, still and silent, the only sound the breathing of our yaks, sleeping nearby. The clouds have moved on, revealing moonlit snow and stars hard and bright as chips of silver. They say there are 3,000 visible stars, but I swear there are three million tonight. Khumbila looms in a spectral glow above me and sends chills down my spine. The peak is sacred to the Sherpas, their patron God on top, and no one may climb it.

As always, the mountain night sky moves me. The Khumbu is about the same latitude as back home, and it's a familiar sky—Orion, the Big and Little Dippers, the W-shaped Cassiopeia at the edge of the Milky Way—but the skies back home don't do this to me. The Sherpas are right. God is here tonight. I need to get to these kinds of places to feel Him, and it doesn't always happen, but He's here tonight. He's in the western wind, He's in the snow-capped peak above me, He's in the temple of the stars. Those stars are trembling, or am I? Get to these kinds of places, Michael, and listen to His voice. It's often a whisper, something inside that affirms you or calms you or warns you or gently prods you in a direction you may or may not want to go. The voice is real, Michael. It's as real and as honest as any you will ever hear. It is Truth, and you ignore it at your peril.

I've reined it in and dive back into the tent. There are still almost four hours before bed tea, and I fall into my first deep sleep in days.

Tengboche (12,650')

*"If only he could get to know the mountains better
and let them become a part of him, he would
lose much of his aggression. The struggle of man
against man produces jealousy, deceit, frustration,
bitterness, hate. The struggle of man against the
mountains is different... Man then bows before
something that is bigger than he. When he does
that, he finds serenity and humility
and dignity too."*
—William O'Douglas

I pop a second antibiotic pill in the morning,
and I'm surprisingly much better. I'm the first
of our group out of the tent, and I'm washing
up and brushing my teeth when Lakpah calls
out, "Ga-ree, come here." (The Sherpas call
me Ga-REE.) Lakpah waves me over to where
he's standing by the stone wall that surrounds

our campsite. On the other side of the wall, across the stream, about 50 yaks of all sizes, colors, and shapes, including some newborn calves, are ambling down the meadow. It's like a Serengeti wildebeest migration and is a cool sight to start out the day.

It's a clear, crisp morning. We're hitting a weather-lucky pattern of clear, glorious mornings followed by cloudy, overcast afternoons. The Sherpas set up a table outside and serve us breakfast under the dramatic backdrop of Khumbila. The sky is a glacier of blue light streaked by a single ray of morning sun splintering through a notch.

"How're you doing?" Andrew asks me.

"I'm a new man," I reply.

"You're amazing," Billie Jean says.

"And cute," I say. "Don't forget cute."

I pass on breakfast, though, not as confident as I sound, and wanting to give the antibiotic a chance to kick in.

Soon after, we start the hike to Tengboche (pronounced TENG-bo-shay) Monastery, the spiritual center of the Khumbu. The

Rinpoche of Tengboche lives there and the area is considered holy and sacred where nothing can be hunted or killed. Expeditions to the 8000m peaks traditionally stop here to receive the blessings of the high lama. We start the trek with a long descent to the Dudh Kosi river, down the river valley to 10,700 feet. It's a beautiful, welcome downhill heading east into the morning sun, and finally firing on all cylinders, I'm feeling light and strong.

On the banks of the Dudh Kosi is a small settlement with several water-driven prayer wheels. We cross the wooden suspension bridge over the raging white water and then begin the two-hour 2,000-foot ascent up through conifer and rhododendron forest to the tranquil ridgetop site of the Tengboche Monastery. I finally find my uphill rhythm and the steep trail is not bothering me, but I hang back with Carolyn. She's struggling mightily against an upper respiratory infection and is gasping for breath. After all I've been through, she's got my sympathies. When Carolyn stops, unable to go on, I ask Sonchai, who's playing sweeper today, to go ahead and get Andrew back here to check her out. I sit Carolyn on a rock and break out a Snickers bar for us.

We're face-to-face with the huge sprawling bulk of Kantega. Together Carolyn and I search for a summit route up the fierce looking mountain face, don't find one, and only half pull off the attempt to distract her. She's in bad shape. Andrew returns and I ask if he wants privacy with Carolyn. He nods his assent. I kneel before Carolyn and lock into her imploring eyes. "Don't give up," I tell her. "Don't back down."

I go off alone on the trail, enclosed by the forest. My stride lengthens. I push myself, reveling in the burn in my legs, the pounding of my heart, the quickness of my breath. My senses are heightened, my mind takes flight. At least for now—for one sharp, glinting moment—I've left everything behind. I'm just a man, one beating heart, alone in an unspoiled realm of peaks, forests, and fast-running rivers. For that brief moment, the gears of the universe click into sync.

I break for a pit stop and wait for Andrew and Carolyn to catch up for the final push to the ridgetop monastery. Sonchai comes back to us with some boxes of mango juice, a thoughtful, touching gesture, and the four of us crest the ridge together. Carolyn touches my arm at the top and croaks out a "Thank you."

Tengboche is all the thank you I need. It's a dreamscape, a surreal monastery atop a huge grassy meadow surrounded by dwarf firs and rhododendrons and one of the world's most sweeping views— Kwangde, Tawache, Everest, Nupste, Lhotse, Ama Dablam, Kantega, and Thamserku in a killer lineup of the Himalayan giants. Kantega means "horse saddle", and from Tengboche it looks so close and inviting that you're ready to saddle up.

The rest of the team is down meadow, sitting at a lunch table waiting for us. Steve is having a Snickers pie he bought at a little stall. I'm tempted to buy a cheeseburger in paradise from the same place, but still playing it safe, opt for just one of Pemba Tzering's pancakes for lunch. I haven't been eating, but I've stayed well-hydrated the last four days, drinking liters of water mixed with Gatorade. Andrew takes Billie Jean with him into a lodge to examine Carolyn. I can see the concern on his face, and I overhear him telling Pemba they may have to make plans to send Carolyn and Billie Jean back.

Pemba has appeared out of nowhere. He left us yesterday to return home when he got word that one of his brothers-in-law had died on Everest. I'm not sure how he covered so much ground so quickly. I touch his shoulder and give him my condolences. "*Ke garne?*", Pemba says to me, Nepali for "what to do", but meaning more like "that's life", a mix of acceptance and resignation.

After a leisurely lunch, we all walk up meadow to visit the monastery, the largest in Nepal. The original monastery was destroyed in an earthquake in 1934 and in a fire in 1989, but it is holy to the Sherpas and has been rebuilt again and again on the same site.

You can see why. The site is a throne room to the mountain gods.

Guarded by stone lions at the base of its steps, Tengboche is a sacred place of humility and serenity "devoted to the worship of the Divine Dharma, the Perfect One". A sign there reads: "May you journey in peace and walk in delight and may the blessings of the Perfect One be always with you." The chapel is brilliantly colored and dominated by a 13-foot-tall statue of Buddha flanked by images of Manjushri, the god of wisdom, and Maitreya, the future Buddha. I watch Pemba prostrate himself before the altar as we enter.

Although it's clouded over, muting the panoramic view from the top of the monastery steps, we linger there anyway, taking photos and talking in hushed tones. We then make our way to a nearby gift shop where Sherpani women are hand-painting beautiful cards. Then we're back on the trail again for a short 20 minute downhill jaunt to our campsite outside a lodge in Dewoche, a quiet little settlement nestled in the velvet afternoon gloom with yak corrals behind it and the spike of Ama Dablam overhead.

We have afternoon tea with yak bells playing a sweet, random symphony around us, then some tent time to rest up and catch up on my journal notes. That evening in the dining tent, I cautiously eat a pasta dinner. It stays down. I'm better at last. We crawl into our tents and settle in for the night about 8:00 PM after a long, satisfying day.

I'm out of our tent in the middle of the night. Diamox and an aging bladder don't mix well. There is frost on our tents, and it's crackling cold standing out in just my thermals. Jackals are howling in the surrounding forest, but the night sky is clear and close, the moon frosted too, the Milky Way a sandstorm of stars. High over the peak of Ama Dablam, a little below the North Star, I make out Cassiopeia, two of the stars in its W-shape among the brightest in the galaxy. Here's a tip, Michael. Remember the story of Cassiopeia when you're out under the stars one night with a special girl. Like all good stories, it begins long ago and far away.

In ancient Greece there lived a vain queen named Cassiopeia, who boasted that she was more beautiful than the daughters of the god of the sea. This angered the god Poseidon. To punish Cassiopeia, he demanded that her daughter, Andromeda, be chained naked to a rock on the seacoast and sacrificed to a sea monster. But the Fates intervened. Perseus, the son of Zeus, returning from his quest to slay Medusa, the snake-haired maiden who turned all who looked into her face to stone, sees Andromeda chained to the rock. He falls in love with her at first sight, saying to her: "The only chains that should bind you, my lady, are the chains of true love." Perseus strikes a bargain with Cassiopeia and her husband, King Cepheus, that if he slays the sea monster, he will win Andromeda's hand in marriage. The sea monster rises from the sea. Perseus battles and slays it, but the vain Cassiopeia reneges on the deal. She, her husband, and their army attack Perseus. His life on the line, Perseus whips out the head of Medusa he carries in a satchel around his waist and turns Cassiopeia and Cepheus to stone. As punishment, the king and queen are banished to the stars, with Cassiopeia forced to hang upside down to teach her humility. Perseus and Andromeda ride off into the sunset together and live happily ever after. When their lives are ended, they join Cassiopeia and Cepheus up in the night sky, their love immortalized forever in the stars.

End of story. Be tender and gentle with that girl. Sweet dreams, my son.

Pangboche/ Chulungche (13,266')

"The mind wants to know all the world, and all eternity, even God. The mind's sidekick, however, will settle for two eggs over easy."
—Annie Dillard, Total Eclipse

Morning dawns clear, crisp, and cloudless. Our tents and yaks are crystallized with frost. The view is epic. Spindrifts of snow are blowing off the tops of Everest, Nuptse, Lhotse, and Ama Dablam. I'm getting into a morning ritual: wake-up bed tea at 6:00 AM, pop half a Diamox, the antibiotic, and a multi-vitamin pill, wash up outside the tent in the basin of washing water the Sherpas bring me, brush my teeth, back in the tent to pack my duffel and backpack, toss them out so the Sherpa crew can break camp, and emerge to a glorious morning, feeling intensely alive, every nerve ending tingling, ready to take on the day.

This morning I eat my first full breakfast since I can't remember when. God, the omelet tastes so freaking good. We're going off the itinerary today, taking it easier so Carolyn, who is really congested and suffered mightily yesterday, has a day to recover. I like Andrew's all-for-one, one-for-all decision.

The trail heads northeast today to the village of Pangboche, the highest year-round permanent settlement in the valley, and there is not much elevation gain. The level trail passes mani walls in a deep rhododendron forest. I watch the leaves, curled up in the cold, uncurl when the morning sun strikes them. Garlands of moss sway sensuously from ancient oaks. I see a musk deer grazing in the fern-covered forest. He is still in the morning mist with a kangaroo-face that stares me down for several moments before he loses interest and bounces away with awkward movements.

Up a slight hill to the left of the trail is a nunnery where I hear the melodic sound of nuns chanting their morning *pujaa*. As a sign outside explains, the nuns are chanting "prayers for the well-being of all sentient beings." Several of our group have already been inside and are leaving as I arrive. Removing my boots, I enter the nunnery and am instantly enthralled. Ten women in saffron robes are sitting in two lines facing each other, chanting rhythmically, their heads shaved, their meal of morning soup before them. Many of the women have runny noses or worse, but their chanting is hypnotic, and I stay, sitting cross-legged, entranced for 30 minutes.

Finally snapping out of it, I slowly stand up, not wanting to leave. I bow in reverence with my palms together at my chest, flash the nuns a smile and get a few back in return. I stuff 200 rupees in the donation box, and when I emerge from the darkened nunnery into the bright sunlight, Sonchai is waiting patiently for me, with the big, radiant smile that perpetually graces his face. We're a good half-hour behind the rest of the team, and I say to Sonchai, "Let's kick it into high gear and catch up." He nods, continues to smile, and we haul ass down the trail. In about 20 minutes, we catch up with the group.

We continue on to Upper Pangboche. Ama Dablam is right in front of us, and I'm feeling refreshed and energized and am in front of the group. As usual, *chortens* mark the arrival into the village, in this case two of them.

We take a long lunch break in a small plaza outside a restaurant while Andrew, Pemba, and Mark go off to inject a village woman's badly swollen, arthritic knee. The woman is the mother of a well-known Sherpa who has summited Everest ten times and is married to an American woman who works with Mark back in Washington State. Mark's co-worker, when learning that our trek leader is a doctor, has asked if Andrew can administer the cortisone shot to her ailing mother-in-law. Mark goes along to bring the woman pictures of her grandchildren. It's a nice gesture. Pemba goes along to translate and finds out he's a cousin to the climbing Sherpa and a nephew to the woman. Your Bubbie is smiling. There are six degrees of separation in this world.

When they return, we're off to visit the *gompa* in Pangboche, the oldest in the Khumbu region at over 300 years old. The *gompa* once contained relics that were said to be the skull and hand of a yeti, but the relics were stolen in 1991—another unsolved chapter of the yeti legend.

Beyond Upper Pangboche, we move through coppery splashes of waning sunlight as the trail winds downhill, crosses the Dudh Kosi again over a swaying suspension bridge, and then rises steeply to our campsite on a windy, exposed plateau at Chulungche. Again, I'm leading the group, taking my energy from the mountains, feeling strong and confident. But hey, it's been an easy day.

As always, tea is at four. The clouds hover

above us, low and gray, a thin film of cold mist turning the air pearl. The temperature is falling fast on the exposed plateau, and I whip out my down jacket and fleece pants for the first time. The gastro-intestinal thing is behind me, but it's bled right into a slight cold. At dinner, we huddle for warmth in the dining tent. Night falls all at once, and by 8:00 PM we're all huddled into our sleeping bags. I read *A Soldier of the Great War* by headlamp, waiting for sleep to settle over me.

Ama Dablam Base Camp (15,400')

"It was an almost perfect cone of snow… so radiant, so serenely poised that he wondered for a moment if it were real at all."
—James Hilton, Lost Horizon

Ama Dablam Base Camp is the objective today, and I've been looking forward to it. It's one of the most beautiful, haunting mountains in the world.

Another cold, crisp morning, the open sky is as clear as can be. Carolyn stays in camp as the rest of us start out with a fierce uphill that climbs from our campsite on the plateau up to a high ridge. I quickly shed my fleece top as the sun rises above the ridge. The going is tough—it's too early for anything this steep—and the uphill takes a lot out of me. I'm thinking the ridgetop will never come, but finally it does, and we level off for a while, heading west through stunning terrain to the Mingbo Glacier. We hit our first snow around 14,500 feet and push on.

Climbing higher, making our way around several bends, we crunch in snow until the trail opens up to a grassy meadow and a mind-blowing sight. We're face-to-face with Ama Dablam, and the sight of it will stay with me forever. Twin white crystal peaks soaring out of the sunlit meadow and glittering against a cobalt sky, not a cloud in that sky, just the sun and the blue, the light phosphorescent and the peaks pulsing with power. I imprint it all and store it deep so I'll be able to bring it back again and again.

It's the peak pre-monsoon climbing season, and there are several small expeditions nestled in the sun-filled meadow. We wander around and meet two young, 20-something climbers from Colorado and one of their girlfriends who is their base camp manager.

I catch myself grinning. The two guys are fearless and full of that all attitude, no brains mountaineering bravado you've got to love. They remind me of the two British brothers in the movie *Vertical Limit* who, when asked to join a rescue party to go after the hero's sister who is stuck in a crevasse near the top of K2, reply with something like, "You want us to speed summit up there? Don't even know her exact location? Frostbite our dicks off? Chances of succeeding are zero? We're in."

We sit and leisurely eat the lunch we've packed in and just stare at the mountain. The Southwest Ridge from Camp Three to the summit is clearly visible from base camp, and my eyes trace the summit route—up that long ridge to the left of a huge hanging ice serac, then the final push to the top. The mountain's name comes from that high-hanging ice serac located just below the summit, which resembles the *dablam*, a jewel box that unmarried Sherpa women wear around their necks— and Ama Dablam is a jewel of a mountain. Andrew, Steve, and Mark decide to make their way up a ridge towards Camp One, but I'm content to just sit quietly and stare in awe at the mountain. There is no wind. A fleeting moment of zen, I drink in the grace and the power and the intoxicating stillness.

We blast our way back down the trail, leaving the shining mountain behind, downhilling to our camp on the plateau on Chulungche. We're flying on the steep down-hills and make great time on the way back. The Sherpas are waiting with hot lemon. A shower tent is set up, and I jump in for a quick one. It feels good to shower off the grunge and be clean again.

Afterwards I just bask in the afternoon sunlight, feeling very alive, until 4:00 PM tea. Jeff and Steve bought playing cards in Namche, and I teach the group Texas Hold 'Em with matchsticks for stakes in the dining tent during tea. There's a lot of cutting up, the competitive spirits kick in, and everyone gets into it. I remember the cinnamon roll I bought at the Namche bakery and dig it out of my pack. It's still delicious, especially dipped in the tea, and I share it around the table.

We have a good dinner and are early to bed as the temperature again drops quickly with the sun fall on the exposed plateau. As night settles around us, I hunker down into my bag, still buzzing with residual adrenaline, thinking *What a day!* When I'm an old man in that rocking chair, this epic climb high, sleep low mountain day is one I'll cherish.

Saturday, April 29, 2006

Bibre (14,500')

"Gravity sucks."
—No Fear Tee-shirt

I wake up still feeling the Ama Dablam high from yesterday. Today will be an easier day, again giving Carolyn time to heal. It's just a four-hour hike northeast to our next camp outside the tiny settlement of Bibre. But it's a great four hours with lots of different terrain and landscapes. Early in the day we hit Dolomite-like terrain, rolling hills of green meadow beneath jagged peaks, which has my mind wandering back to those fairy-tale mountains in Italy, and later on a lot of rock hopping among expanses of boulder gardens.

We spend some time bushwhacking through thorny barbary bushes along the banks of a burbling stream, then we ascend a steep ridge and contour along it with the Imja Khola running fast and clear below us. We descend to its banks, cross it just below a pretty waterfall, and make our way up to our campsite in a stone-walled yak corral alongside the trail between Dingboche and Bibre.

Because of the short hike, we've beaten our porters and yaks to camp today. I unshoulder my pack, rest it against a stone wall, and just lean back on it looking up at the clouds and the mountains above us. We've crossed to the other side of Ama Dablam now. Its north face, Island Peak, and Tawoche all tower above us. As I lay there, I can't remember the last time I just stared up at the clouds and watched them morph from one shape into another. The porters and yaks are not far behind. I watch them unload, just shaking my head at the immense loads that the porters carry. Feeling guilty just sitting there, I help the Sherpa crew set up our tents.

Lunch is served on an open tarp, and afterwards Andrew asks for a volunteer to demonstrate the *gamow* bag (pronounced GAM-off) used for treating AMS (Acute Mountain Sickness). No one is stepping forward, so I do. I crawl into the airtight bag with Steve foot-pumping me oxygen. Everyone is gathered around watching as I hold Andrew's altimeter up to the plastic window in the bag as it drops me from 14,500 feet back down to 8,800 feet. I use the scuba equalizing technique of pinching my nose and forcing a sneeze as the pressure inside the bag gets to me. As I get out of the bag, Pemba jokes that I just went back down to Tok Tok. I feel some rapture of the deep, like I've just been diving.

I spend the rest of the afternoon reading and catching up on my journal. We play a long game of hearts at tea. It's a variation of the game we play with the Jack of diamonds taking you down ten points. The team is mostly novice players, passing all their high cards, so I keep trying to shoot the moon. I do twice in a row at the end of the game to win it. They all think I'm a card shark.

Pemba Tzering serves us a good stir-fry dinner, and as always, as twilight deepens, we're in our tents early around eight. My cold has morphed into a dry, persistent cough that Andrew calls a "Khumbu cough". It stays with me for the rest of the trek and for weeks after I get home.

Chukhung (15,584′)

"I will lift mine eyes unto the hills,
from whence cometh my help."
—*Psalm 121, a song of ascents*

We're staying in our camp outside Bibre
another night, and today is a welcome exploration day. We all need a rest day to shake our
various ailments. I've got the kind of cough
that can crack ribs, and my nose is running
like a faucet. I'm popping cough drops and
going through tissues like there's no tomorrow.

We sleep in an extra hour, eat a leisurely
breakfast, and start off, eastward into the
morning sun, on the classic Khumbu day hike
to the small summer settlement of Chukhung.
When we left Pangboche a couple of days
ago, we left the last permanent village. We've

been in true wilderness since. These little settlements are nothing more than one or two trekker lodges.

Blue sky reigns and it's a beautiful hike with 1,000 feet of gradual elevation gain through moraine fields surrounded by massive glaciers. We pass through the tiny settlement of Bibre and about two hours later, after passing some yak trains and crossing several streams, we cruise into Chukhung.

Three of the guys decide to continue onto Chukhung Ri, a steep ascent of over 2,000 feet to a rock outcrop with a view of Makalu, Ama Dablam, and Baruntse. But the view from the outdoor café where we've stopped in Chukhung is so stunning—the moraine fields of Island Peak, the great south face of Lhotse, the picturesque eastern face of Ama Dablam, and straight ahead the immense fluted ice walls of Amphu Lapcha, an 18,785-foot mountain pass—that I'm content to just sit back in the warm sun and take it all in.

I order a delicious piece of apple pie (spelled pai on the menu), a cup of hot chocolate, and three packs of tissues. Not like me to pass on climbing a peak, but the day is meant for relaxing, my ribs hurt from coughing, and all the hard stuff—Kala Patar, the Cho La, and Gokyo Ri—is still in front of us.

We re-trace our steps back to camp with the views even prettier heading west. A shower tent is set up again after lunch for the rest of the group that didn't catch one at Chulungche. Andrew is lounging around camp in shorts after his shower, and the cook boys spot a huge tick on his leg, probably from the bushwhacking we did yesterday. They spend about 15 minutes diligently rubbing it out with a home-made solution that removes it intact.

We play another spirited game of hearts but I'm not into it, too distracted by the sun melting on the horizon. It touches the serrated edge of one of the higher peaks, breaks like yolk, and streaks the sky blood orange. We take in a fantastic pizza dinner and the last light. Maybe I'll open a chain of Pemba's Nepalese Pizza Parlors when I get back. The pizza is that good. I spend a restless night tossing in our tent, my sleep wracked with bizarre altitude dreams, the cold and cough working on me.

Monday, May 1, 2006

Duglha (15,100')

"I want a kiss from your lips,
I want an eye for an eye,
I woke up this morning
To an empty sky"
—Bruce Springsteen, Empty Sky, a song of 9/11

We've been looking down into Dingboche and up at the daunting hill leading from it for the last two days. This morning we head there. It's a gorgeous morning, and it's a beautiful trek down into Dingboche, a pretty village with some wake-up Vivaldi playing from one of its lodges.

I'm feeling strong, and the hill leading out of Dingboche that looked so intimidating turns out to be pretty easy once we're on it. A picturesque *chorten* and prayer flags greet us at the top, and I stand on a small dirt pad where I saw a helicopter land earlier in the morning and take in a fantastic view. Island Peak is aptly named, and in the distance to its right, over a pass, is the greenish-gray peak of Makalu. The Imja valley is below us, and before us lies a long, wide open plain of high yak pastures surrounded by silver mountains with icefalls at their bases.

As we cross the plain, my body goes into autopilot, and my mind drifts away into a dreamy, meditative state where I lose all track of time. I snap back to attention when the trail climbs onto the terminal moraine of the Khumbu Glacier, demanding concentration, and starts crossing small streams on gleaming boulders. We're entering what is purported to be snow leopard and yeti country with Tawoche and Cholatse hulking overhead.

We contour down to a stream, cross it on a bridge with a waterfall above us, then head up to the Pumori Lodge in Duglha where we're camping for the night. Big bearded lammergeiers circle in the updrafts above us as we eat lunch on the outdoor patio of the lodge, and I catch a glimpse of a lone eagle soaring on a wind current. There's a ridge above our campsite with superb views of Cholatse, Tawoche, and Lobuche Peak.

Snow starts falling lightly in the afternoon. We go into the lodge for tea, play a long game of hearts, and stay through dinner while the snow continues to fall. The lodge is packed with trekkers from Belgium, France, Italy, and New Zealand, and the conversations flow around the iron stove, warming the gloom of the lodge. English is the universal language here, and it's cool to hear it spoken in all the different accents. We hear that snowfall has detoured some trekkers' plans and that this week six Sherpas have been killed on Everest.

One of the posters tacked to a wall of the lodge is of the skyline of Manhattan, pre-9/11, before the empty sky, the twin towers of the World Trade Center still standing tall. It casts a haunting quality to the already eerie scene. Snow is still falling when our headlamps guide us to our frosted tents for the night.

Lobuche (16,200')

"Climb the mountains and get their good tidings.
Nature's peace will flow into you as sunshine flows
into trees. The winds will blow their own freshness
into you, and the storms their energy, while cares
will drop away from you like autumn leaves…
Of all the paths you take in life,
make sure a few are dirt."
—John Muir

I'm out of the tent at a pre-dawn 5:15AM
to catch the sunrise. The snow has stopped,
and the sky has cleared. Another cold, crisp
morning, a few stars still hanging onto the
sky. In my down jacket and fleece pants, I
climb to the top of the ridge behind the lodge
and watch the dawn light up the mountains
one by one. Andrew is already there with his
camera and tripod. Carolyn is feeling better

and is on the edge of the ridge doing yoga sun salutations while Andrew snaps away. The mountains are aglow in the soft palette of morning light.

I go into the lodge and hang with a bunch of Sherpas, warming up and drinking tea around the iron stove, then eat a pancake and honey breakfast.

The trail from Duglha starts with a steep one-hour ascent up the lower end of the Khumbu Glacier to the top of a ridge, under prayer flags, and into a large field of lateral moraine known as Chukpilhara. Stone monuments stand along the crest of the glacial moraine overlooking a mist-filled valley, memorials to climbers, many of them Sherpa, killed in the area, most of them on Everest. Two large *chortens* memorialize Scott Fischer, one of the nine climbers killed on Everest in the disastrous 1996 Into Thin Air climbing season, and Jangbu Sherpa who was killed one year later. I stand before another monument with a Star of David and Hebrew writing on it, dedicated to Terence Stokol, a Jewish climber who also lost his life in the Khumbu.

An eerie stillness rests over the area. At its far end, I climb a small, snow-covered overlook and watch the team wander among the ghosts of Everest. No one is bulletproof here.

The trail drops a little and enters a long, easy, flat moraine that continues all the way to the yak grazing pastures of Lobuche. We're on a broad valley floor, hugging the western side of the canyon wall. To the east is the glacial moraine, a 12-mile tongue of ice that flows down from the south face of Everest, and flanking the moraine in the distance is another canyon wall of mountains.

At 16,000 feet, we've left behind the last vestiges of green. We're in Everest country now, and although the mountain is not visible, I can feel its presence. I intentionally drop behind the group, lost in my thoughts and the serenity of the valley.

Pemba is the sweeper today. I ask him the name of the lodge we're staying at in Lobuche and tell him to go ahead of me. "No problem," I say. "I'll follow the yak dung all the way to Lobuche." Pemba nods his assent and leaves me alone on the trail. I soak in the solitude and the deep tranquility of the canyon and fall into another trance that I don't snap out of until I hit the outskirts of Lobuche.

Andrew has described Lobuche as "a good place to get sick", and Jon Krakauer's depiction of it as a "spectacularly filthy" cesspool with human waste running down its dirt streets is indelible, but fortunately we've hit the settlement at a quiet time, and our lodge, the Eco Lodge, is relatively new and clean. I arrive there still feeling the high of the meditative trance and join the rest of the team for some hot lemon on the porch.

After lunch, I catch a long hot shower. I do a double-take at my suntanned, newly-bearded face in the mirror, do some repair work on that all-too-gray growth, change into my last clean clothes, and settle in with my book and journal on a comfortable bench in the glass-enclosed dining room of the lodge. I shake my head as two Israelis enter the lodge, argue with the Sherpa owner about the rate

($18 a night), and storm out in protest when he won't come down.

We play some hearts, and just before sunset when the sky starts thundering and lightning, I grab my headlamp and jacket and head outside into the bracing air. The light show over Lobuche raises goosebumps. My thoughts are all of tomorrow when we go for the summit of Kala Patar, at 18,400 feet, the highest point we will reach and the place I intend to bury the Livestrong wristband for Jon. I know I'll be thinking of Jon all the way to the top.

I'm riveted as the lightning flashes around Nuptse, leaving a silver frieze around its summit, and I figure at a time like this, a prayer to the mountain gods can't hurt. In the fading light of the cold dusk, with snow pellets bouncing off my down jacket, I pray for clear skies in the morning and for the strength and the will to get Jon and me to the top.

I get back to the lodge and dry off for dinner in front of the iron stove. Later, even though I'm in my first bed after six straight nights of camping, I'm filled with the sense of dread I always feel before a summit, that shiver of fear in the face of overpowering nature, and I know I won't get much sleep.

Kala Patar (18,400')

"Climbing is not a battle with the elements,
nor against the law of gravity.
It's a battle against oneself."
—*Walter Bonatti*

"I believe that no man can be completely able to
summon all his strength, all his will, all his energy,
for the last desperate move, till he is convinced…
that there is nowhere to go but on."
—*Heinrich Harrer*

Game time. I wolf down some oatmeal and a cup of joe, and we hit the trail at 6:30AM heading northeast into the morning sun. First prayer answered, it's a crystal-clear morning. The day radiates excitement. We follow Lakpah up the western side of the broad Khumbu valley and ascend gently through meadows alongside the glacial moraine. The ascent becomes steeper and rougher as we cross the rubble of the Changri Glacier, still active under the moraine.

After two hours, we round a bend, and in the distance, we can make out the Lho La, the mountain pass in Tibet where George Leigh Mallory looked into Nepal in 1921. He named it the Western Cwm. To the west of the Lho La stands the conical peak of Pumori. On its lower slopes, a ridge extends to the south and terminates in a small peak. This is Kala Patar, Hindi for "black rock", but from this vantage point it appears more brown than black and deceptively easy.

We descend down into Gorak Shep, a sandy, flat dry lake landscape straight out of a Mad Max movie. Gorak Shep was the base camp for the unsuccessful Swiss Everest expedition of 1952. The successful British expedition of 1953 called it "lake camp."

We stop outside of the lodge in Gorak Shep where we'll be camping after going for the summit of Kala Patar.

The sun is strong overhead. I peel down to my lucky Mountain Hardware zip-T and put on suntan lotion and lip balm. If I had face paint, I'd put it on, too. I take several long hits of water, pop a cough drop, refill my water bottles, and lighten my pack as much as I can. Locked and loaded, it's time to go for the top.

We head north, crossing the sandy floor of the dry lake. On its far side are two trail signs, one pointing west towards Kala Patar, the other east towards Everest Base Camp. We follow the western trail, heading up the grassy slopes at the base of the peak, and start for the summit. The trail is steep, "a good grunt" as Andrew calls it.

The verticality soon separates our conga line, leaving each of us alone with our thoughts. I'm breathing evenly, in time with a mantra and my locksteps. Pemba, Andrew, Sonchai, Jeff, and Steve are ahead of me. The others are behind.

After an hour of straight up climb under a blazing sun, my walk has lost its bounce.

Come on, I tell myself, *Kili's summit was an 18-hour ultramarathon, a lot harder than this.* The little voice inside my head answers, *Yeah, but you were eight years younger and stronger.*

An hour later, the grassy slopes are gone. It's just rock now, and the strength of my chant gives out. It's replaced with a new mantra: *Stick it out.* Stick, as in hang, as in no retreat, no surrender. I'm wasted. It feels like every ounce of energy has been sucked from my muscles.

Up ahead of me, incredulously, is a large group of Indonesians, led by a woman on a horse. The horse cannot handle the steep trail. It keeps stopping and starting, and the group has the narrow trail totally jammed. I detour off it to pass them, and whatever I have left is gone.

I'm drained and running on nothing but sheer will power now. That little voice inside is imploring me to dig deeper and pull this one out for Jon. *One goal at a time. Just make it to the next switchback, the cairn up ahead, the pinnacle in the distance. One lockstep at a time, one foot in front of the other. Fight through the fatigue. Never, never, never quit.* Beyond the physical now, it's become a mental game, an ultimate character test, the mountain and me, as simple as that. No way I'm giving in. I have not come all this way to bail now, and Jon won't let me.

Mercifully I see a snow-covered shelf ahead strung with prayer flags, and my heart soars. But when I make it there, the flags are just a tease. It's a false summit, but the shelf is level, and I thank the mountains gods for that. For a moment, I'm not sure which way to go. I've lost sight of the team ahead of me, and when I look back, the rest of the team is far behind. Then I see Sonchai appear in the distance to my right. He's waving at me, and even from this distance, I can see his ever-present smile. *Good old Sonchai,* I smile back. *What would I do without you?* I crunch in the snow along the ridge to where Sonchai waits for me.

The trail jags around a cornice, and then, above us, looms the final pitch to the summit of Kala Patar. It's a steep, snow-covered, rocky outcrop, and Sonchai wants to lead me up it. I wave him off, telling him I can handle it. The temperature has fallen dramatically, and I pull a pair of thin climbing gloves from my pocket, put them on, and start the scramble to the top. Sonchai follows. It's good rock, but there's exposure here on the open face, and I start to get that queasy feeling in the pit of my stomach. *Don't get gripped,* I tell myself. To avoid it, I do what I always do. I block out everything except solid handholds and footholds and go up as fast as I can.

I'm on pure adrenalin now and before I know it, I'm on top, where Andrew, Pemba, Jeff, and Steve are huddled together on a windy ledge with prayer flags flying around them. *We made it, Jon.*

"How long have you guys been here?" I ask.

"Only five minutes," Andrew answers. "You were very fast on that last pitch, mate."

"That was pure fear," I say with a smile, still sucking air.

Sonchai pops up on the ledge 15 seconds behind me, as breathless as I am. We high-five each other, and he motions to the true summit, about 30 feet up a stiletto ridge above. I stare at the summit and swallow hard, but we both go for it immediately. Pemba yells out a "Be careful." The pucker factor is high with the exposure here. We should be roped up for this, not free soloing it, and it's an all-fours scramble to the summit. Sonchai is soon jumping up and down on the narrow point at the very top with his 23-year-old exuberance. I look down and see Andrew and Pemba shaking their heads. I reach up a hand to steady Sonchai. He misunderstands and starts pulling me to the top where he's standing. There's no room for two of us.

"No, Sonchai," I yell into the wind. "Let's live to climb another day." I point downwards. He sees the menacing stare he's getting from Pemba, and we scramble back down.

"My fault," I say. "We won't be doing that again." I remind myself that there are old climbers and bold climbers but no old bold climbers.

Sonchai hands me a cup of hot lemon from a thermos he brought for us to the summit, and as I bring my pulse and breathing back under control, I realize for the first time how cold I am. I pull on a fleece jacket, trade my baseball cap for a fleece hat I pull down over my ears, and take in the view while I wait for the others to make it to the top. They do, about ten minutes later, each with a Sherpa in front extending their hand every step of the way.

There are high-fives all around and a rush of emotions—some tears, some hugs, some laughs. Then, after gathering for the obligatory group summit shot, I know it's time. As the others watch, I walk off alone across the ledge to a rocky outcrop, kneel on its edge, and peel off the Lance Armstrong wristband.

Goraks, Himalayan ravens, circle around me and cry out. I bury the wristband beneath a pile of rocks and build a cairn for Jon. My throat clogs, my eyes tear, I'm a mess of emotions. *I'll remember you, Jon. I will remember.*

The vista before me is surreal. The gray peak of Pumori streaked like a watercolor, the Lho La Pass leading into Tibet, the enormous faces of Lhotse and Nuptse, and behind the twin guardians, rising above a swirling cauldron of clouds and towering over all, the South Face and West Ridge of Everest, Chomolungma, the Mother Goddess in full glory, her summit pyramid an ink-black shark fin soaring into the sky, a haloed crown of ice crystals streaming from her top like a scarf of frozen smoke.

There it is—the summit of Everest, the site of so much striving and tragedy, that's haunted my dreams since I was a kid. From the top of Kala Patar, the summit is still more than two mind-bending vertical miles above us, and India is still pushing under Asia moving it up a quarter inch a year.

A group hug greets me when I rejoin the team. Carolyn and Billie Jean see my tear-streaked face and start sobbing.

"There goes my tough guy image," I say. The two of them shake their heads at me, too.

Reluctantly, we leave the vista and start the long downhill back to Gorak Shep. I smile watching Sonchai take off, scampering down the mountain, his arms spread, a winged monkey flying fearlessly down the steep slope. I'm brought back to rapt attention when Mark, who is directly in front of me, snaps one of his trekking poles, starts a slow-motion pirouette that takes him off the trail to the edge of the cliff, and just catches himself before taking a bad spill.

"Hey, no off-roading," I kid Mark. "Stick to the trail."

Mark is OK but badly shaken. He's over-cautious the entire rest of the trek.

For me it's a sweet downhill after the bite of the ascent, the pain forgotten, feeling a strange mixture of summit exhilaration and a melancholy for Jon. I'm out front but thoroughly whipped when I get to the Mad Max landscape at the bottom of the peak, cross it alone, and head up to the lodge where we're camped. The Sherpas greet me with a basin of washing water. I pour it over my head, go into the lodge, and drink a liter of water while waiting for the team to make its way back for lunch.

I keep expecting to start shaking, to get hit by some racking adrenaline drain now that I'm safely back at camp. Instead, I feel fantastic, quiet, my mind and body calm with fatigue, feeling more alive than before. The Sherpas bring me lunch. *What am I doing? Why am I here? I'm a grown-up, a husband, a father, a grandfather. I'm 57 years old, for Christ's sake.* But the cup in my hand is not shaking, and the lunch tastes sublime.

We continue the hearts tradition at tea— we're all dialed into a rhythm to our days that no one wants to break—and hang in the lodge until dinner.

That night, in our tent, Mark shares his thoughts. "I cried with you today," he says softly. He confesses that the day rocked him and tested his limits.

"That's a good thing," I say gently.

Mark's not so sure. Silence falls as fatigue does, with stealth and force, and we both drift off.

The night is cold. Good and cold. The water freezes in our Nalgene bottles. When I clamber out of the tent in the middle of the night, the mountains are shrouded in the clouds, lying in wait for the morning. After a day like today, so am I.

Thursday, May 4, 2006

Everest Base Camp (17,600')

"The highest mountain in the world, the ultimate mountaineering trophy, has become accessible to sort of ordinary Walter Mitty types with a spare 65,000 bucks."
—*Jon Krakauer*

We're off to a 7:15AM start, re-tracing our steps from yesterday to the trailheads across the dry lakebed of Gorak Shep. This time we follow the trail sign east towards Everest Base Camp.

It's about a six-hour round trip from our camp. Early on, at the crest of a ridge, we come upon stone monuments remembering the climbers killed in the 1996 climbing season and signaling a grim warning of what can lie ahead. I spend some time before Rob Hall's memorial. He led the ill-fated '96 team and died at the top of Everest, no strength left after getting caught in a storm and riding out a sub-zero night. The satellite phone call he makes to his wife, who is seven months pregnant with their first child, is incredibly moving. They choose a name for their child before he dies. It's the ten-year anniversary of the tragedy this week. I've got to re-read Jon Krakauer's *Into Thin Air* when I get back.

There's not a lot of altitude gain on the trail to base camp, but just to walk in the footsteps of Hillary, Mallory, and Irvine is reward enough. The going is tough along the rubble-encrusted Khumbu Glacier, the glacier alive and active underfoot so the trail is ever-changing. Lakpah uses my hiking stick several times to draw arrows in the dirt to help the stragglers in our group find their way. It's a barren, monochromatic moonscape of rock and wind-blown ice, alien and dreamlike. The vista is still, vast, apocalyptic.

The walk seems endless. It rolls along,

sometimes between boulders the size of houses littered on the moraine, sometimes on the glacier itself. A new trail veers above and to the left of the old one where the famous 40-foot-high ice seracs stand guard over the glacial valley. Overhead is the *whump-whump-whump* of a helicopter on its way to a rescue mission.

As we enter base camp, we're greeted by another helicopter, an off-kilter wreck downed in a crash last year, another stark reminder of the dangers ahead. Up here the air is so thin the blades sometimes have nothing to bite into.

Base Camp is a domed city, a sea of brightly colored tents and prayer flags. Training ladders are mounted above imitation crevasses to allow climbers to practice walking across them in crampons. Snow crystals swirl and sparkle in the wind. I hear the roar of an avalanche overhead and far below the cracking of the glacial moraine, a deep interior fracturing sound. The stress of the mountain runs through me.

Base camp is an eastern valley far below

Everest. We can't see the mountain, but we can feel it. We are within its aura.

There are 35 expedition teams in camp. We wander in and talk to several of them. Everest Base Camp hospitality is legendary, and the teams we talk to don't disappoint. We're invited into the tent of Team No Limits from Colorado. The Everest community is a small world. When I was standing in front of the mirror two days ago in the lodge at Lobuche, trimming my beard, I was talking to a doctor from Tennessee named Larry Rigsby who was on that team. He had come down with HAPE (high altitude pulmonary edema), had hung up his climb, and was making his way back to Lukla. Roger Coffey, the team's cowboy-hatted base camp leader, is lamenting how tough that was for Larry since the summit meant everything to him. Andrew rails at the CEO climbers who just view Everest as another trophy, and later comments to me that if you want the summit badly enough, you don't hang it up that easily. You go down, recover, and then try again.

The commercialization of Everest, as Krakauer hammers home, has changed the mountain forever. The real adventure is gone. Before every season, teams of Sherpas run ladders and ropes to ease the climbers over the tough parts, and any CEO in good shape with $65,000 to burn has a reasonable shot at summiting if the mountain gods deliver good weather. As I'm writing this journal, the Everest controversy continues. Reports are trickling out that days after my return, 40 climbers walked right past David Sharp, a British climber collapsed on the trail and desperate for oxygen, and let him die, unwilling to risk their own summit attempts. Hillary called it "horrifying". Faced with attempting to save a life or attempting to bag a trophy, there is no choice. Yet 40 climbers didn't see it that way. So much for the morality, ethics, and style that mountaineering has long championed. So much for compassion and altruism. The new breed of trophy-bagging climbers, the outfitters who need high success rates to warrant their high fees, and "real" mountaineers who have to summit to retain their sponsors have all combined to create a perfect storm that has devastated real mountaineering on Everest.

The mountain has gotten zooed. The glory days are gone.

Still, as we're leaving base camp, I look longingly up at the Khumbu Icefall, the frozen river that flanks the camp and starts the climb up Everest, and as we're trudging back to the lodge at Gorak Shep, I steal several longing glances backward.

Lunch is waiting at Gorak Shep. So is Mark. He makes me laugh with his story. Early on the way to base camp, Mark just doesn't feel up for it and returns to our camp with Sonchai. As they're walking back, Sonchai asks him, "How old are you, Mark?" "Fifty-three," Mark replies. Sonchai nods knowingly and says, "No wonder."

Everest Base Camp was our northernmost point, and we're starting our way back home. Snow pellets start falling from the slate sky, and I haul ass back to the Eco Lodge in Lobuche where we're spending the night again, cutting a two-hour walk to 90 minutes.

Later in the lodge that night, I leave Mark alone in our room to recover from an altitude headache and join Andrew and Pemba in the dining room around the iron stove. In the still and quiet of the night, Andrew fights back tears and unloads the story of the death of his friend and climbing partner on Makalu two years earlier. The anchored bolt that holds for Andrew moments before pulls out of the wall when his friend attempts the same move, and William falls 2,000 feet to his death on a ledge below.

The relived agony of climbing down to the shattered body and meeting with William's family to tell them of the death is too much for Andrew. As shadows leap on the wall of the lodge behind him, Andrew finally loses it. Tears spill down his face. I watch them glitter in the dim light and listen to Pemba's chant which starts as a hum, becomes a hymn, and ends as a dirge.

Dzonglha (15,900')

"In wildness is the preservation of the world. We simply need that wild country… For it can be a means of reassuring ourselves of our sanity as creatures, a part of the geography of hope."
—*Wallace Stegner*

A dense morning fog envelopes Lobuche. We wait an hour in the lodge for it to lift, hitting the trail at 8:30AM. A silvery mist still hangs in the air as we descend south along the lateral moraine of the Khumbu Glacier with Zomba leading the way.

Veering right off the main trail, we leave the glacier and traverse along the side wall of the canyon. We hit a couple of short, fierce uphills that bother me but take us above the mist. Mostly we're ridge running with the

Imja Khola river valley below us and stunning pastoral views all around.

Turning a corner onto a small plateau, we come face-to-face with Cholatse and Tawoche, an awesome panorama with Ama Dablam further off on the eastern horizon. We take a rest stop and soak in the view before continuing our ridge run on the muddy trail.

We're getting into wild country and soon the Cho La becomes visible through a notch in the distance. The Cho La is an imposing mountain pass covered in permanent snowfield. It can be dicey, and it's the part of our trek that has concerned Andrew the most. From the eastern side which we'll be ascending, there's a glacier crossing that, in bad weather conditions, requires an ice axe, crampons, and roping up to get over the icefall at the foot of the glacier. If that's the case, our team won't be attempting it. But in ideal weather conditions, there are no technical problems and there is a trail of sorts in the rocks beside the icefall.

The pass is too steep for our yaks to

cross, and we've sent them on a longer, lower altitude trail via Pangboche and Phortse to Dragnak where we'll meet them tomorrow afternoon on the other side of the pass. We've also pared our gear down to one duffel for two people so our porters can handle the load over the high pass crossing.

We hit one last uphill that takes us to Dzonglha, a flat shelf of land near a yersa, a summer yak herders' settlement, beneath the north wall of Cholatse. We stop there for a long lunch with impressive views of Ama Dablam to the east and the majestic Baruntse up the Imja Khola valley. Then we wrap the day with an hour trek to our camp which lies beneath the notch leading up to the Cho La.

In typical fashion, the sky clouds up in the late afternoon, and we wait out a hard rainfall in our tents, resting up for the Cho La tomorrow and hoping for clear skies in the morning.

Cho La (17,783')/ Dragnak (15,500')

"When I'm finally there, up high, breathing in the sky… exhausted and scared and hopeful and pushing upward with an electric joy coursing through me, it is as if the mountains and I were made for each other."
—Mark Jenkins

The mountain gods must know it's Rachel's birthday. They're with us again. We wake to a bluebird day. It's a sparkling clear, warm morning, a naked sun in a cloudless sky.

We couldn't have ordered more perfect weather for the Cho La. I eat light. Adrenaline is the breakfast of champions today, and mine is off the charts. At 7:45 we're crossing the flat shelf of land that leads to the notch up to the pass. A tremor of excitement rolls through me.

The notch is steep, it's slow going, and when I take my first water break, I look back to see our campsite far below in the distance. We've gained a lot of altitude quickly, and the verticality has again separated our team.

More heads-down, just go for it uphill before I'm emerging out of the rocky notch onto the permanent snowfield. My breath is taken away in every sense of the word. The pass is wide open and beautiful, a vast field of snow rimmed with glaciers and snow-capped mountains, glittering in the sunlight like uncut diamonds.

It feels like real mountaineering as I ascend the snowfield. This is thrilling country. Off the trail, there are crevasses all around. When we were kids, we would say that if you fell into one, you'd fall all the way to China. The Sherpas say that if you fall into a crevasse, you'll fall all the way to America.

The sun glares strongly overhead in a China blue sky and it reflects also off the snow underfoot, and soon, despite the high altitude, my first layer is an even sweat. I get in a zone as I crunch my way up the pass, losing myself in the stillness and the beauty.

Amped up, a rock star today, I'm the first of our team to get to the base of the glacier. Sonchai is right behind, ice axe in hand. This is the crux, the glacier crossing that can get hard-core in tougher conditions. Sonchai starts chiseling steps out for us with his ice axe. I shake him off. "We've got this," I say. I take the lead. The real-deal no-shit climbing has me laser-focused on the scramble up the icefall. I hit my groove on the long, steep pitch, and when we top the glacier, I nod and have this moment of, *Yeah, I get why I do this now.* On top of the icefall up high under the pulsing sun, Sonchai and I are there, exhaling.

Three roped climbers, silhouetted against the azure sky, are slowly making their way up to the summit of nearby Lobuche Peak. "Us, next year, Ga-ree?", Sonchai asks. "You're a mind reader, Sonchai," I answer.

Sunlight ignites the glacier, sparking fire and ice, a moment of quiet elation, a craving for more.

The climbers on Lobuche Peak trigger Sonchai's thoughtfulness. He grabs a coil of rope from his pack, we anchor it, then send it down to help the others make it up the last 60 tough feet. Steve joins us with a "Gnarly". "Cool, awesome, intense", I answer Sonchai's quizzical look. When the team is all together at the top of the icefall, we high-five and forge on.

The snowfield levels off for a while and then ascends a final time to the top of the prayer-flag strung Cho La pass. I step up onto it with a whoop.

It's spectacular at the top with cascading icefalls around us and a new western vista into China with the peak of Cho Oyu and the Ngozumpa Glacier unveiled. There is no wind, it's warm, and we linger over Snickers bars and photo shoots, basking in the satisfaction of knowing we've just knocked off the hardest part of our trek.

The Cho La is a saddle between the Khumbu and Gokyo valleys. The descent down the other side of the pass into the Gokyo valley is steep and treacherous. The snow is slick now in the late morning sun. I'm right behind Sonchai who is leading us down and futilely trying to chip out steps with his ice axe. I angle my way slowly down the slippery sunlit slope, almost ass-planting once, and finally the snow changes to loose scree and the going is a little easier as we reach the bottom of the high pass crossing.

We've descended into a Garden of Eden. The valley floor is lush from the snow run-off of the pass, and we're boulder hopping through a primal lost world landscape. The boulder hopping catches up to Billie Jean, who goes down behind me, badly turning an ankle. Pemba is with her, and she limps her way to our lunch stop. I wrap her ankle in an Ace bandage while we wait for the porters to catch up with our supplies. They're only about 15 minutes behind us. I marvel at the half-men, half-mountain goats who negotiated the Cho La Pass with those enormous loads on their backs. Our team gives them a standing ovation and, for once, we serve them some hot lemon.

After lunch, we ascend a steep ridge with a huge boulder at the top, and then it's a beautiful downhill coast, following the river to our camp outside the Cholaview Lodge in Dragnak.

A large mountain goat, a *tahr*, stands motionless on a ledge above, like the mystical White Buffalo in the *Rin Tin Tin* episode of my childhood, staring down at us as we set up camp.

Beyond the Ngozumpa Glacier, Machhermo Peak and Gokyo Ri fill the western sky. As that sky turns steel gray, we go into the small lodge with a blanket for a door for afternoon tea and later huddle around the stove for a well-earned dinner.

With tired legs but a content mind, I read in our unzipped tent until the gray dusk melts into purple night and the land blends with the sky. Rach, I hope you celebrated your 31st birthday in style. I sure did.

Sunday, May 7, 2006

Gokyo (15,600')/ Gokyo Ri (17,600')

"Find beauty, be still."
—W.H. Murray, mountaineer-mystic,
after being released from years spent
in German and Italian POW camps

It's a two-hour trek crossing to the western side of the massive Ngozumpa Glacier, the largest glacier in the Khumbu, which sweeps down from Cho Oyu and leads to Gokyo. The trail first rolls along a dry lakebed, sandy and white in the sun, then leads into a stunning glacial wilderness that is dotted with pristine glacial lakes, some frozen, others calling out for rocks to ripple their surface. I answer the call.

On the other side of the glacier, we enter

the Gokyo region, a quiet, pastoral valley with five turquoise glacial lakes. An easy, level walk, we follow the valley past the second lake known as Taoche Tso, and then a boulder-strewn path up to Gokyo, a serene little settlement, almost like a summer resort, with stone houses and walled pastures along the shores of the third, large lake known as Dudh Pokhari. This is a holy lake to the Sherpas, and no one is allowed in it. We make camp outside of a lodge above its shores. Cho Oyu towers to the north and the peak of Gokyo Ri is directly above us.

We've got a choice to make. The easier option is to continue along the trail to the fifth lake, Ngozumpa, with its ridge view of Everest, called the "scoundrel's view" because it involves no hard work. The harder option is the two-hour straight up climb to the summit of Gokyo Ri. The view from the top is said to be one of the world's most incredible mountain panoramas. Easy call. *Whenever life presents you with two paths, choose the harder one.* Andrew, Jeff, Steve, and I cross the valley floor just to the north of the lake and head for the summit.

It's a tough climb as we switchback our way up the barren trail. About halfway up, I'm moving in slow motion and lagging behind. Even worse, I can see thick, dark thunderheads starting to roll in from the north and I can feel the air turning juicy. *No choice,* I tell myself. *Kick it into high gear. Or get soaked and shut out.* Like a jockey spurring on his horse, I whack my hiking stick against my thigh and will myself to give it everything I've got. Racing the clouds now, my heart revving, my lungs on fire, I join the rest of the team on the snowless summit under the prayer flags flying at the top at 17,600.

Ducking between the crisscrossed strings of prayer flags, I climb atop a boulder and overlook the world. All is right with the universe. The Ngozumpa Glacier spills down a broad valley like a frozen river. The sapphire waters of the Dudh Pokhari glitter below. And four of the six highest peaks on the planet sweep across the sky. The dome of Cho Oyu

crowns a long white wall. Makalu knifes sky-
ward. Lhotse rears but is dwarfed beside the
huge black rock pyramid of Everest. The feel
is primeval, other-worldly, a face-to-face intro
to divinity. It doesn't last long. The wind roars
off the ridge, clouds roll in, and it starts grap-
pling—Andrew's Aussie word for the snow,
ice, and rain combination that's pelting us. We
all get our rain gear on and scramble down the
mountain. I'm fast and strong on the downhill, and Andrew and I get to the lodge ahead
of Jeff and Steve, peel off our rain gear, and
dive into the waiting lunch.

I spend the rest of the afternoon recover-
ing in the lodge dining room, my adrenaline
tapped out after the climb. I look out at the
sacred lake and up the trail to the peak of
Gokyo Ri, now lost in storm clouds. I listen
to the quiet, peaceful sound of the rain on
the lake and the low din of the dining room
full of trekkers from Europe, Canada, and
New Zealand as I finish reading *A Soldier of
the Great War* and work on my journal. Our
two yak herders, both very pretty Sherpanis,

come in out of the rain and stand by the warm
stove. They are too reticent to take chairs, so I
bring them both one. They give me shy smiles
in return.

Brent, as usual, is talking to everyone in
the lodge. Andrew waits his turn to take on a
Slovenian woman in chess and wins the match
to the amazement of her companions. Pemba
sits next to me and sees the frayed bookmark
with your picture on it that you made me
for Father's Day long ago. Proud fathers that
we both are, we talk about our kids. He's got
three daughters in a private boarding school
in Kathmandu who he dearly misses, and
a young son, still at home in his village in
Phortse, where we're headed tomorrow. Then,
still sitting next to me, he starts chanting
under his breath while rolling prayer beads in
his hands and falls into a trance.

Later outside our tent in full night,
I'm spellbound, too. The moon lays down
a wide silver path across the sacred lake.
Constellations wheel across the sky, and most
bewitching of all, moonbeams spill down,

etching the summit of Gokyo Ri in a spectral radiance. Blood ticks electric through my veins as I remember the view from the top. Earth as seen from heaven.

The last of the hard challenges is behind us now. We're going off the itinerary tomorrow, trekking to Pemba's home village of Phortse, starting the long hike back to Lukla and back home.

Monday, May 8, 2006

Phortse (12,500')

"It's a round trip.
Getting to the summit is optional,
getting down is mandatory."
—Ed Viesturs

The Dudh Pokhari, the third sacred Gokyo
lake, mirrors the golden form of Cho Oyu in
the morning sun. It's our last sight of Gokyo
as we head back down the valley, through the
terminal moraine of the Gokyo glaciers, and
start the long trek home.

As we pass the second Gokyo lake, one
of our pretty yak herders, Andiki, runs past
us on her way back home to Khumjung, her
arms extended by her sides, running wild and
free like a little girl down the pastoral valley.
She flashes me back 23 years to Rachel as an

eight-year-old, running carefree after a flock of sheep on the meadow shores of Lac Bleu, high in the mountains over Chamonix. Those flashbacks to long-forgotten things in your life, vivid and real again, are precious gifts from the mountain gods.

We pass the trail where we entered the valley yesterday after the glacial crossing and soon come to the first lake, Longponga Tso. A family of ducks has lived here for years. A simple wooden bridge beyond the lake leads us down a narrow staircase trail. Below us water rages over boulders bleached white by the river as the clear water from the Gokyo lakes joins the glacial outflow from the Ngozumpa Glacier. Above us a veil of mist hangs in the valley below the glittering peak of Thamserku. I'm thinking this is the prettiest stretch of trail we've hit yet.

The trail takes us down into the Dudh Kosi gorge, the river thundering below. We boulder hop across the swollen river, then it gets wild and wooly as we contour our way up from the gorge along the glacial moraine to Na, the only year-round settlement in this part of the valley. From there, we hit a couple of uphills, but we're mostly cruising downhill and mountain rock is changing into green meadow.

Lunch is at a small lodge in Thore, a village of stone-walled yak corrals, little stone buildings, and emerald pastures right out of medieval England. It's a hobbit's shire and I'm half-expecting Bilbo Baggins or Frodo to come waddling around a corner to greet us.

We leave Thore and soon climb to a large *chorten* under prayer flags on a high ridge top. From this vantage point we can see Phortse across a verdant valley on a distant ridge. A lone yak is roaming free above us, his broken reins trailing behind him. We descend to Phortse with red and white rhododendrons in full bloom along the trail as we get to lower altitude.

Phortse is a beautiful, classic Sherpa village, cradled in mountains. The village is set in a terraced bowl. A cleft valley flows out of the bottom of the bowl to the horizon.

Twin peaks—Thamserku and the sacred Khumbila—soar majestically above. We get there at 3:30PM after seven and a half hours on the trail. It's been a long day but a good one as we downhilled 3,100 feet from 15,600 at Gokyo to 12,500 here at Phortse. I was in cruise control for most of it, pampered by the oxygen-rich air, gulping it down, and inhaling all the green around me. Life and I are breathing fully again.

A pale sun hangs on the horizon as we make camp besides a small lodge on a terrace at the top of the village. Pemba goes home to surprise his wife and son and soon returns with two smudged-faced kids—his five-year-old son, Nima, and sidekick little girlfriend, Diki. Sherpas traditionally name their kids for the day of the week on which they were born—Nima is Sunday, Lhakpa is Thursday, Pemba is Saturday. Diki is heaven-sent, already telling Nima what to do and how to act, and in this small village of 400 people, I can already see they're destined to marry and grow old together. My thoughts turn to Mom and you. I'm going to miss all this, but it's good to be on the way home. All day long, a new mantra has played inside my head: *Khumbu road, take me home, to the place I belong.*

Tuesday, May 9, 2006

Exploration Day, Phortse (12,500')

"A man does not climb a mountain without bringing some of it away with him and leaving something of himself upon it."
—*Sir Martin Conway*

We wake up to roosters and birdsong, the picture-perfect medieval village spread below us, the smell of livestock and fresh bread. The sun has yet to come up. It remains hidden behind the mountains, its sharp light glancing off distant peaks. In shadow, red-tailed pheasants wander around our camp, unafraid because all wildlife is sacred to the Sherpas, and they know they will not be harmed.

It's an R&R day in Phortse. Pemba joins us and leads us up to the new monastery at the very top of the village. A work in progress, 12 years and counting under construction, but the *gompa* is very meaningful to the village, and Pemba is very proud of their accomplishments. New bronze prayer wheels adorn the front, and I give them each a spin. A lone monk is inside hand-painting the altar and the walls and ceiling. Every inch will be covered with Buddhist iconography, and there is still a long way to go.

A heavy mist rises from the valley as we walk back to camp. It starts to lift a while later as we make our way down the terraces to visit the village school. I stare in enchantment at Phortse. The village is immaculate, a beautiful quilt with squares of green meadows separated by stone walls, each square with a little stone house and carefully tended rows of barley and buckwheat, all balanced, serene, classic.

The school has three small classrooms, no heat, no electricity. We watch the kids playing in the schoolyard. They start their day in military fashion with exercises, grouped in three lines by age, and following in time to a whistle blown by one of their teachers. Nima and his girlfriend are in the youngest group and bring a smile to my face. Diki's in perfect time, Nima is clueless.

The kids used to sing a song of allegiance to King Gyanendra to start their day, but that's history now. While we've been on trek the last 18 days, the king has been overthrown and power relinquished back to the Parliament and the people. It's enough to make you believe in solar eclipses and whack job ancient astrologers.

Pemba takes us to the little two-room health clinic around the corner from the school. There are no patients this morning.

We've time-traveled hundreds of years back to another place in time, a time when we still felt awe at pure and simple things, the changing of the seasons, the blooming of a flower. A time almost, but not quite, lost.

Our group scatters in different directions. I go off alone, wanting the solitude, slowly zigzagging my way back up the manicured terraces to our camp at the top of the village. Far in the distance a lone mountain *tahr* is moving with spooky ease, sure-footed across a nearly vertical granite face.

There's a serenity and a clarity here in Phortse, a Shangri-La feel in this timeless place. This is what we want from our mystical kingdoms, isn't it? Places where we find a surer, more ancient pulse and the harmony and the purity the best of us endlessly seek. I'm somewhere deep inside, and I stay lost in that place for an hour.

An afternoon of Caribbean "liming", just leisurely hanging out, and then we all walk down to Pemba's house for afternoon tea. Pemba's home is warm and inviting. There's an altar in the main room, and the walls are full of family pictures and academic and athletic awards his kids have won. Pemba and his wife, a gracious and graceful Sherpani, serve us Sherpa and black tea and delicious chips (fries). Pemba also brings out some *chang*, the Sherpa moonshine made from rice or barley. Pemba ignores Andrew's request for a half-glass and fills his glass to the brim. I take a hit of Andrew's. The citrus taste is not bad, but the gastro-intestinal wounds are still fresh. I stick with the tea.

As we're leaving, Pemba's wife presents us with white *khatas*, blessing scarfs of silk with the *mani* prayer and Buddhist symbols woven in, that she places around each of our necks. "For good luck," she says. "Our way to wish you a good life." It's a touching farewell gesture.

Back at camp, we watch a tie-dye sunset light up Thamserku before thunder rumbles and the clouds start rolling in from the valley below. The clouds slowly ascend towards us, casting an eerie light. It looks a lot like the Angel of Death scene from *The Ten Commandments* and feels like it, too.

The team spooks and scurries for the small lodge. I stay, alone on the high terrace waiting for the mist to swallow me. It rushes up the valley now, and soon the village below is gone in a total whiteout. I stand transfixed in the clouds, rooted by something ethereal. "Take care of Jon," I whisper to it.

A hard rain falls most of the night, battering our tent and breaking my sleep.

Monjo (9,250')

"Why do I do this?
Because if I don't, I go fucking crazy."
—*Conrad Anker on Meru*

Morning. We get off to a 7:45AM start down through Phortse and down a slippery trail through flurries of red, white, and pink rhododendrons dripping with night rain and morning dew. We cross the bridge at Phortse Tenga, then climb 1,000 feet, flowing through mists and old-growth forest to the top of the Mong La at 13,000 feet. The last killer ascent of the trek, I take it slow and unhurried, lost again in a reverie.

At the top of the pass, we hang a left and traverse along a short ridge to an overlook with an astounding view across the valley of much of the ground that we have covered over the last 19 days. Andrew comments reflectively, "This was not a trivial trek."

We continue on a pretty balcony trail, contouring through lush green forests, up and down steep stone stairs, past a beautiful hillside *chorten* all the way to Namche Bazaar.

After an almost five-hour walk, we return to the huge rock covered with white Sanskrit inscriptions that signals the downhill to Namche. Andrew, Jeff, Steve, and I detour to the Panorama Lodge where we stayed earlier in the trek. We're welcomed with hot lemon on the house. Jeff and Steve buy *thanka* paintings that they regretted passing on 16 days before.

We wind our way down to downtown Namche. At the Hermann Helmer bakery, I slam down a cheeseburger and fries, devour an apple strudel, and we all pick up some gifts from the shops outside. I look around at our group. We are not the same people who were here over two weeks ago.

Rain sheets down as we're leaving

Namche, a hint of the coming monsoons that will end the climbing season. We don our rain gear and slog our way down Namche Hill in the cleansing rain. This is the hill that almost wiped me out on the way in, but there's a serene smile on my face as I surf down it, blissed out, looking into the tense faces of the trekkers making their way up.

We navigate some bridge crossings over the Dudh Kosi, the river running clean and white. Our permits stamped at the guard station, we bid farewell to Sagarmatha National Park and make our way to our last camp besides the trail in Monjo. Twilight settles like a murky veil as a wet wind whips through the village. We spend our last trail dinner huddled together under the dining tarp, feeling something slipping away beneath the night blue sky.

Lukla (9,350')

"I don't know who was the conqueror or who was conquered. I do recall that El Cap seemed to be in much better condition than I was."
—Warren Harding

The wind dies during the night, leaving Monjo still and bright in the morning. I'm up at 5:00AM after an unwelcome wake-up call from a wacky group of Indonesian women doing exercises right outside our tent. It's the same crazy group with the woman on the horse that I had to detour around on the summit climb up Kala Patar. Lucky for them, I'm in a Buddhist state of mind.

Our last bittersweet day on the trail, we're retracing our steps from the first day on the trek, coming full circle back to Lukla. We're staggered on the trail, leaving camp at our leisure. I'm walking with Jeff and smiling at the incredulous faces of the Sherpani women in the villages as they take him in. At 6'8", Jeff is a Gulliver in their land. Billie Jean and Carolyn catch up to us. "You're cute, Ga-ree," Billie Jean jibes in her Southern Sherpa accent, "but Jeff is the one they're gawking at."

About two hours into the walk back, we regroup and take a long detour up into a lush green paradise through sets of wooden gates to see the Rimjung *gompa* that Pemba has never before seen. Worth the detour, it's the prettiest monastery we've visited all trek.

Back on the trail to Lukla, the sky blackens and a sudden squall bombs down on top of us, a direct hit, shredding our visibility, its glistening rain pellets stinging us and leaving us chilled and shivering. It blows off quickly, but the rest of the team jets off. I fall behind, refreshed and unfazed by the rain, slowly meandering up and down the rolling trail, crossing bridges, passing *bhattis* (tea shops) and *mani* stones, cruising from one Sherpa village to the next, not even trying to catch up. It's that Buddhist state of mind.

The gray skies clear. A rainbow arches across the horizon, yanking me from my reverie, as I top the last hill and make my way into Lukla. I wander down the dirty, shop-lined alley that is main street Lukla with no idea how to get to the lodge where we're staying but too laid back to be concerned. I finally see Andrew and Pemba standing outside a shop. The others are inside shopping.

Andrew smiles at me and says, "Did you join a monastery back there, mate?"

"Thought about it," I say, smiling back. "Just didn't want this to end." Andrew and Pemba both nod their understanding.

We wind around the airstrip to our lodge passing propellers, wheels, wings, and other pieces of crashed planes. Not too comforting.

The generator in the lodge has blown. We have some hot lemon and lunch around the stove in the dining room, but when it becomes apparent that the generator won't be fixed, we grab our gear, trudge uphill, and check in the Numbur Lodge that overlooks the airstrip runway.

I stay in the shower of our bathroom for 30 minutes, soaping up, rinsing off, doing it again, then clean at last, make my way upstairs and meet Andrew in the lodge dining room. I'm totally drained, feeling great, thinking about nothing other than dinner and a beer, not in that order.

"I'm done with asceticism," I say, smiling at Andrew.

"I'm done with afternoon tea," Andrew replies, in sync with me.

I buy Gurkha beers for both of us, click my bottle to his, and thank him. There's nothing like that hot shower and cold beer, well-earned after 20 days of roughing it.

There are no flights coming or going in the misty gray late afternoon. Andrew and I knock down our beers and begin our prayers for clear skies in the morning so we can get out of here.

Our Sherpa crew prepares an excellent roasted chicken with potatoes for dinner and an apple cake dessert. After serving us, they sit at an adjoining table and eat *daal bhat* with their fingers. We've made piles of gear for them and do a lottery drawing to give them out. The Sherpas are very appreciative, flashing us their world-class smiles. Andrew gives them a thank-you speech, stopping to let Pemba translate, and hands out the tips we've pooled for them.

Pemba then turns to us. "There have been many groups canceling," he says. "We prayed that you would not, and you answered our prayers." We stand and applaud them. Without their support, we would have never made it.

Zomba leads the crew in Nepali and Sherpa dancing, and soon they've got us all up joining in. Their smiles and laughter are contagious. We're not sure if they're laughing with us or at us, since our dancing is not quite ready for prime time, but it really doesn't matter. It's a nice way to say farewell. The Sherpas can go all night long during their festivals, but we're not in their league. Around 11PM, we say goodnight and head to bed. We've got a 4:00AM wake-up to catch that first flight out of Lukla back to Kathmandu.

Friday, May 12, 2006

Kathmandu

"This ain't no lunar disco."
—The Cuban Cowboys, from
a Talking Heads song

It was a crapshoot whether the morning
mist would clear for us, but it does, and
we're on the first Yeti Airlines flight back to
Kathmandu. Pemba returns with us to see his
daughters in their boarding school and to get
a visa to the United States so he can do summer landscaping work in Oregon. He places
golden *khatas* around our necks as we board.
Again, the mountain gods are shining down
on us. Our flight is the last flight out of Lukla
for the next two days.

   Far below the icy peaks of the Himalayas,
Kathmandu lies basking in its warm,

subtropical valley. It's in the mid-80's when we land around 10:00 AM, and life in Kathmandu is back to its normal, frenetic pace. The utter mayhem of the strikes and protests is over, and the streets are again teeming and chaotic. The city is frozen in time, still the trippy hippie mecca it was back in the '60's and '70's.

We check back into the Shangri-La Hotel, and I call Mom. It's 1:00 AM back home, but I know that we both need to hear that everything is all right. After reassuring each other, Mom tells me that Jon was readmitted into Johns Hopkins Hospital and is dying.

In a daze I wander down to the hotel lobby. I find a postcard with the view from the top of Kala Patar and write Tim, Lollie, and Jon to tell them that I left the Lance Armstrong wristband on its summit for Jon. I leave the postcard at the bell desk to be express-mailed.

Most of the team meets in the lobby, and I lead them into Thamel. We have lunch at an Indian restaurant and then we scatter. Billie

Jean and Carolyn go off on a shopping frenzy. With a three-week growth, I go off in search of a barber shop. I find one down a little side alley, and for the princely sum of 100 rupees ($1.40), I get the best shave of my life. I wander out of Thamel, picking up tee-shirts, a mask, and some crafts for gifts.

A chocolate shake by the hotel pool and a long shower later, I meet up with the group and we catch two taxis into Thamel for a much-needed pizza and margarita dinner at a place called Fire and Ice. On the open-air patio, I take in the day's last glow, the dying sun sending its final flares across the coral sky, and I can't help thinking of Jon.

I'm eating a soft chocolate *gelati* for dessert as we walk through the narrow streets of Thamel back to the hotel.

A full moon hovers over Kathmandu, and in the garden in the back of the hotel, I drink a *sambuca* and take in a band playing '60's stuff—the Doors, Hendrix, Cream. The night shakes my memory and sweeps me back, like Kathmandu, to that frozen time—a time before you, before Rachel and Abby, before almost everything. The moondance and these last ten life-shattering weeks inevitably make me reflect back on my life—the things that drove me, the decisions I made, the mistakes I regretted, the people I cherished. I find myself asking, like Private Ryan 40 years later: *Did I do the right things? Was I a good man?*

Kathmandu

"Doesn't everything die at last, and too soon? Tell
me [my children], what is it that you plan to do
with your one wild and precious life?"
—Mary Oliver, "The Summer Day"

"Every man dies. Not every man really lives."
—William Wallace in the movie Braveheart

At 9:00 AM we leave Kathmandu and cross
a broad, polluted valley to tour Bhaktapur,
"the city of devotees", an ancient city of
huge cobbled squares, Hindu temples, and
medieval palaces about 20 miles southeast of
Kathmandu. Now a city of potters, painters,
and sculptors, there's great architecture, most
of it dating back to the late 17th century, with
erotic Kama Sutra-type woodcarvings on some

of the buildings, golden roof finials topping others.

As we're gallivanting around the town, we're stopped by dragons and a long parade celebrating the 2,500th birthday of Buddha. It's an auspicious day, the halfway point to Buddha's alleged 5,000th year return as Maitreya, the future Buddha and messiah.

The air vibrates with henna-faced yogis stirring metal singing bowls and the hypnotic sounds of *bhajans*, devotional songs, echoing against redbrick walls. In Durbar Square, boys launch bamboo and paper kites off the temple steps, then race down into the open square to tug them into the sky. At the far end of the square, the horizon is carved with the distant peaks of the Himalayas, majestic, holy, seeming almost in reach.

Back in Kathmandu, the rest of the team heads back to Thamel. I head out to Mike's, a well-known climber's hangout in a section of town called Naxal, for lunch and a beer.

There's a good art gallery upstairs from the courtyard restaurant, and I get the rest of my shopping done—a bronze casting of a monkey for our sunroom, another casting of a dancing Buddhist goddess for Mom, a mandala *thanka* painting, and a statue of Buddha as a gift to Pemba for the new Phortse monastery.

I catch a taxi back to the hotel and an hour by the pool in the late afternoon sun.

Later that evening as I'm walking into the Lost Horizon bar in the hotel lobby, I'm hit with an overwhelming feeling that Jon has died. I feel Jon come into me, and I'm sure of it. I order a Macallan 18, the best single malt scotch in the house, and raise my glass to Jon.

It's not how you wanted it, Jon, but you're at peace now. In my mind's eye, I see you on the other side, in the *bardo*, smiling at me from a mountain top, prayer flags flying around you. *I'm not sure you're really there, Jon, but I like to think so. I hope so. Om mani padme hum, Jon. Om mani padme hum.* The ancient Tibetan mantra captures the essence of Buddhism—the end of suffering.

Our farewell dinner is at the Third Eye restaurant in Thamel. The steak and the camaraderie are good, the fellowship of the rope still strong. But I'm somewhere else. Jeff reads a goofy poem he's written about our three weeks in the Khumbu. Andrew takes out his laptop and shows us the edited version of the photos he's been shooting all trek. Andrew is a well-published adventure photographer, and the photos are fantastic. He gives each of us a CD with the collection and an 8x12 group shot from the top of the Cho La. We thank Andrew and Pemba for everything they did. I give Pemba the Buddha gift, and he is overcome with emotion.

I'm overcome with something, too, as I walk alone through the streets of Thamel back to the Shangri-La. I can't shake the sense of pervading loss. I've lost the battle rhythm of our days in the Himalayas. It's already gone, and the loss is palpable. The business I built for 27 years is gone, too. I've lost it, and I will miss it. Most of all, I mourn for Jon, and for Tim, and for Lollie.

The adventure is over. It is time to get home. Home to your sisters and my grandchildren, home to you and Mom. I can't wait to kiss each of your faces. I guess I've always known that's where the real Shangri-La is.

Sunday, May 14, 2006 – Monday, May 15, 2006

Home

"Home is the sailor, home from the sea And the hunter, home from the hills."
—Robert Louis Stevenson

Jeff and Steve are heading out early to catch a flight to the jungles of Chitwan, and the three of us meet for a goodbye breakfast. The rest of us are all on the same 1:40PM Thai Airways flight from Kathmandu to Bangkok. I finish packing, settle my hotel bill, and walk the gardens in the back of the hotel a final time. I walked these gardens the first time that second night in Kathmandu, loose and confident, looking forward to what lay ahead. Now, after three weeks of searching in the mountains, I'm still unsure what lies ahead. *Was I a sojourner here, just another in a long line of meaning-seekers?* But my mind is clear and untroubled. The mountains have centered me and realigned my internal compass like they always do. I am restored. Whatever lies waiting, I'm ready for it.

Our team is lingering in the hotel lobby, waiting for the shuttle transfer to Tribhuvan International Airport, when Pemba comes in to see us off. Again, he presents us with golden *khatas,* placing the blessing scarves around each of our necks as a final goodbye.

The others, all before me, bow to Pemba with their palms together at their chests, but when Pemba places the *khata* around my neck, I do the Western thing and hug him. When we let go, he touches his forehead to mine.

At the airport, we pool our remaining rupees for some snacks before boarding the flight to Bangkok. Brent, Billie Jean, and Carolyn are spending a couple of days in Bangkok. Andrew, Mark, and I are headed our separate ways home. I've got a tight one-hour connection to catch my next flight to

LA, but luckily the plane leaves on time, and as we takeoff, I take a last longing look at Kathmandu.

At the arrival gate in Bangkok, we exchange some too quick goodbye hugs and handshakes.

"Figure out what you want to do when you grow up?" Caroline jibes.

"Going over to the dark side", I joke. "It pays better."

Andrew and I bump fists. "You've got the glow," he says to me. "Keep your fire burning."

"Roger that," I reply. A final "Adios" to the team, then I turn and hustle to the other side of the terminal to the LA departure gate.

There was no need to hurry. The flight leaves 30 minutes late.

Fourteen hours flying time to LA, I'm out of stuff to read, and after seeing every movie worth watching, it's hard to escape reflecting back and committing philosophy. A month of awe and grandeur in the mountains of Nepal will do that to you.

Michael, in the end, climbing mountains is an inner journey. Mountains are a forge. They show us what we're made of. Every man owes it to himself to put his body—and his heart—on the line to find out what his limits are and to feel what it's like when he pushes beyond them. The glory is not in bagging peaks; the real glory is on the inside. Heinrich Harrer of *Seven Years in Tibet* fame called the Eiger "the supreme testing place of a man's worth as a human being." Don't argue with Heinrich—he was one of the toughest guys who ever lived. Win in that testing place, and you will know you can win anywhere.

In the mountains, and in life, you will always confront adversity. Meet it with courage and grace. Overcome it with grit and perseverance. Be like water. Whatever the obstacles, find your way over, under, and around. Call audibles, whatever it takes. But be like stone, unyielding when your deepest beliefs are on the line.

In climbing, and in life, it's not reaching the summit that matters. What matters most is being bold enough to go for it. So, get gone. Hit the road. Get into trouble. Go where your passion takes you. Seek the "thin places", those extreme landscapes on the planet where the borders between worlds are at their most fragile, those edges where you can reach out and almost touch the other side. You'll find them on mountaintops, under desert night skies, on remote ocean shores. Or in bars in Kathmandu.

Fortune favors the brave. Sure, fear is always there—it's a survival instinct—but don't let it paralyze you. Learn how to manage it. Theodore Roosevelt said: "The credit belongs to the man who is actually in the arena… who, at the best, knows the triumph of high achievement, and who, at the worst, if he fails, at least fails while daring greatly, so that his place will never be with those cold and timid souls who know neither victory nor defeat." No arguments with Teddy either—he was even tougher than Heinrich. If you are worthy, the summits will come.

Be kind along the way to the top. Be

a *mensch* in all things. The truest men are tenderhearted, even if they don't talk that way. Women and children first. Shelter the curvy and protect the small.

Nobody gets out of life alive, Michael. Father Time is undefeated. Before He comes knocking and you're walking through the valley of the shadow of death, make sure that you have lived.

Thou shalt live a life that matters. Yes, it's a commandment, Michael. I put it in Biblical terms to scare you into listening. Live consciously. Your destiny is in your hands. Control it, or someone else will.

Embracing religion is optional, living by a moral code is not. But find a greater purpose—it's what will get you higher than you ever thought was possible.

Balance your rational, scientific mind with the poetry, the danger, and the freedom you will find in the mountains. When you hear the siren of the wild, answer the damn call. Never give up the quest for wonder and magic, for romance and honor, for the sublime and the transcendent. When it's all said and done, leave behind a legacy of love and a life of consequence. We can still leave footprints in a trail whose end we do not know.

Don't be afraid of death. Living in the face of it sets off a cascade of appreciation and realization. Death is the force that shows you what you love and urges you to revel in that love while the clock ticks. Your body will do what a body does, but if you love deeply and well, that kind of love will live beyond you. That kind of love is your path to immortality.

We're late getting wheels down in LA, and even later when we get stuck on the tarmac waiting for a China Air flight to back out of our arrival gate. The good news is I'm back in the USA. The bad news is I miss my connecting redeye to BWI and end up spending the night courtesy of Thai Air at a Four Points hotel outside of LAX. I'm on the 8:45AM flight out the next morning, homeward bound.

Before I know it, there you are meeting

me at United baggage claim, an inch taller than when I left. I hug you and kiss you and place a white *khata* around your neck.

I grab my expedition bag and you shoulder my backpack. Mom is waiting curbside. Her face explodes with light and the radiant smile that always melts me. I hug and kiss her—a little longer than you—and place a golden *khata* around her neck. You are both burning brightly and beautifully.

Whenever I return from climbing mountains, I see life so clearly, and I know that living with you and Mom, simply and in love, is a great thing.

Wednesday, May 17, 2006

Epilogue

"And the end of all exploration will be to arrive where you started and see the place for the first time."
—*T.S. Eliot*

Two days after returning home, I attend Jon's funeral with Mom. It's a standing room only Catholic mass, very moving and touching. Jon's friends give some pretty funny and irreverent eulogies, flasks out. The priest shakes his head, but Jon would've approved.

At the end of the service, Jon's younger brother Bryan delivers his eulogy. At its conclusion, he takes out a postcard. Bryan explains that I went to Nepal, joking that if he went on vacation it would have been Hawaii. Bryan tells about his father's summit ask of me the day before I left for Kathmandu. He ends his eulogy by reading the postcard I sent to Tim, Lollie, and Jon the day Jon died:

"Summited Kala Patar for you on May 3rd. Jon was with me every step of the way. Prayer flags fluttering in the wind at the top, I honored your wish and buried the Lance Armstrong wristband for Jon under a cairn of rocks. There were tears in my eyes. Face-to-face with the Lhotse/Nuptse wall and behind it the mythic South Face and West Ridge of Everest. Some say it is the best view on the planet. Enjoy it for eternity, Jon."

I hear people crying all around me. Bryan looks up at me and chokes up. I nod back and feel my own tears come and my heart break.

Let me end this journal with a story for you, Michael. It's the story of Jamling Norgay, the son of Tenzing Norgay, the Sherpa who did the first summit of Everest in 1953 with Sir Edmund Hillary. Forty-three years after his father's legendary feat, Jamling is part of a three-person 1996 Everest IMAX team going for the summit. One of Jamling's partners,

Ed Viesturs, is probably the best climber in the world. He's summited Everest before, but his goal this time is to do it without bottled oxygen. His other partner, Araceli Segarra, is playmate material, a Spanish rock climber attempting to become the first woman from her country to reach the summit. But Jamling is not climbing for fame or fortune. His motives are pure. As a young boy, he would light butter lamps to ask the mountain gods to protect his father at the top of the world, and he always felt a hunger inside to live up to his father's legend. Jamling is climbing to honor the memory of his father.

It is a week after Rob Hall and eight other climbers have lost their lives on Everest. The team is stuck in summit base camp, the wind conditions preventing any attempt at the summit. But finally, there is a weather break, and the team goes for it. The going is hard for Jamling. Every oxygen-thin breath burns his lungs like cold fire, but his mission is sacred, and he is determined. He searches his soul and summons the strength, and when he makes it to the top of Everest, he kneels and leaves a toy his young daughter has given him and a picture of his mother and father. He has done it. He has honored his father's memory. His heart is overflowing, and his tears freeze to his cheeks. Then, through the winds at the top of the world, he hears his father's voice calling to him, "Jamling, my son, you did not have to come such a long, hard way to find my soul. For I was with you all along."

Just as I will be for you, Michael, my son.

END

Acknowledgements

To my team of Apprentice House Sherpas-
Sienna Whalen, Rosie DiTaranto, Bri Rozzi-
my sincere gratitude for summiting this one
with me.

To my daughters, Rachel and Abby, their
significant others, Michael and Marc, and to
Michael, my son- I did this for you. Take care
of my *kokoro*- it lives on through you.

To my grandchildren- Emma, David, Elijah,
Max, and Tali- for the pure joy you each bring
to my life. You each know who Zadie loves.

And to Iris, always the North Star in my night
sky, always my undying love.

About the Author

Gary Ingber is the former founder and CEO of Open Road Technologies, a software design and development company, and is currently doing public service consulting for the U.S. government. He is still climbing the peaks and diving the reefs whenever he can. Father of three, grandfather of five, Ingber lives outside Baltimore with his understanding wife, Iris.

Apprentice
House Press
Loyola University Maryland

Apprentice House is the country's only campus-based, student-staffed book publishing company. Directed by professors and industry professionals, it is a nonprofit activity of the Communication Department at Loyola University Maryland.

Using state-of-the-art technology and an experiential learning model of education, Apprentice House publishes books in untraditional ways. This dual responsibility as publishers and educators creates an unprecedented collaborative environment among faculty and students, while teaching tomorrow's editors, designers, and marketers.

Outside of class, progress on book projects is carried forth by the AH Book Publishing Club, a co-curricular campus organization supported by Loyola University Maryland's Office of Student Activities.

Eclectic and provocative, Apprentice House titles intend to entertain as well as spark dialogue on a variety of topics. Financial contributions to sustain the press's work are welcomed. Contributions are tax deductible to the fullest extent allowed by the IRS.

To learn more about Apprentice House books or to obtain submission guidelines, please visit www.apprenticehouse.com.